T5-CFQ-769

Legal Services for the Poor

Recent Titles in
Studies in Social Welfare Policies and Programs

Social Planning and Human Service Delivery in the Voluntary Sector
Gary A. Tobin, editor

Using Computers to Combat Welfare Fraud: The Operation and Effectiveness of Wage Matching
David Greenberg and Douglas Wolf

Poverty and Public Policy: An Analysis of Federal Intervention Efforts
Michael Morris and John B. Williamson

Social Work: Search for Identity
Leslie Leighninger

Social Security After Fifty: Successes and Failures
Edward D. Berkowitz, editor

LEGAL SERVICES FOR THE POOR

A Comparative and Contemporary Analysis of Interorganizational Politics

MARK KESSLER

STUDIES IN SOCIAL WELFARE POLICIES AND PROGRAMS, NUMBER 6

GREENWOOD PRESS
NEW YORK • WESTPORT, CONNECTICUT • LONDON

Library of Congress Cataloging-in-Publication Data

Kessler, Mark.
Legal services for the poor.

(Studies in social welfare policies and programs, ISSN 8755-5360 ; no. 6)
Bibliography: p.
Includes index.
1. Legal assistance to the poor—United States.
I. Title. II. Series.
KF336.K44 1987 347.73'17 86-27138
347.30717
ISBN 0-313-25508-3 (lib. bdg. : alk. paper)

Library of Congress Catalog Card Number: 86-27138
ISBN: 0-313-25508-3
ISSN: 8755-5360

First published in 1987

Greenwood Press, Inc.
88 Post Road West, Westport, Connecticut 06881

Printed in the United States of America

The paper used in this book complies with the Permanent Paper Standard issued by the National Information Standards Organization (Z39.48-1984).

10 9 8 7 6 5 4 3 2 1

In Memory of
ROBERT KESSLER
1922–1984

CONTENTS

FIGURE AND TABLES

FIGURE

TABLES

ACKNOWLEDGMENTS

I have accumulated more than my share of debts during the years that this book has been in preparation. I owe a tremendous debt to the nearly 200 individuals who agreed to participate in this study. Because I assured them I would not identify anyone, my appreciation must be expressed to them as a group.

The research was aided by a grant from the National Science Foundation (Grant No. SES8111984). The Institute for Policy Research and Evaluation at Pennsylvania State University provided invaluable administrative and clerical support during my field research. I would like to thank Irwin Feller, the Institute's director, along with Greta O'Toole and Mary Jane Johnson for their assistance during the initial stages of this project. Bates College provided me with a course reduction to write the book. Doug Hodgkin, chairman of the Department of Political Science, generously rearranged my teaching responsibilities so that I could deliver the manuscript on time. Claire Schmoll and Carmen Bartlett typed the manuscript and refused to get annoyed or induce guilt when I submitted more revisions.

When I first considered this study, Bruce Williams and Jim Eisenstein listened to my ideas and posed challenging questions that helped clarify my thinking. Robert Friedman, Dan Katkin, Bruce Murphy, Tom Weko, Jim Rogers, Susan Pearlstein, and Steve Kessler also provided helpful comments. Christine Harrington read the study when it was in its early stages and offered excellent suggestions for organizing the book. I owe a special debt to Jim Eisenstein, my teacher and friend. He has taught me much of what I know about empirical research. His enthusiasm for the scientific enterprise is infectious and it carried me over some of the inevitable "lows" that accompany a research project such as this. At each stage of the project, he offered just the right mix of constructive criticism and praise.

Finally, I would like to acknowledge the support of Rae Kessler, Stephen and Dorothy Weko, and Mindy Morrison, all of whom provided me with a warm house, good food, and stimulating conversation during several of my field visits. I wish to thank my wife, Stephanie, for her unqualified praise and encouragement throughout this project and our son, Bobby, for teaching me that there is more to life than revising chapters.

Portions of Chapter 4 first appeared as "The Politics of Legal Representation," in volume 8 of *Law & Policy*. Extended quotations from articles in the *American Bar Foundation Research Journal*, *Administration & Society*, and from *Research in Law and Policy Studies: Volume 1*, edited by Stuart Nagel and published by JAI Press, Inc., are used with permission.

Legal Services for the Poor

1

INTRODUCTION

While serving as governor of California, Ronald Reagan expressed his anger with the activity of one group of government-funded poverty lawyers, accusing them of "ideological ambulance chasing."[1] Commenting more generally on the national program funding these lawyers, Vice President Spiro Agnew asked: "Isn't it possible that we have gone too far when the federal government constructs a program which encourages individual lawyers to test at public expense their own individual theories of how the resources, rights, and benefits of that society should be distributed among the population?"[2] More recently, North Carolina Senator Jesse Helms charged that "the Legal Services Corporation has festered into a gaggle of political activists run amok."[3] Echoing these sentiments, conservative political activist Phyllis Schlafly lamented that the "Legal Services Corporation . . . has turned into a monster which is fomenting radical and revolutionary programs at the taxpayers' expense."[4]

As these statements reveal, government-funded legal services programs for the poor have been immersed in political controversy for most of their history.[5] The controversy rages despite little empirical evidence regarding their operations and daily activities. This book seeks to shed empirical light on the continuing controversy by answering some central questions raised by the quotations above: Are criticisms of poverty lawyers and legal services programs justified? What do LSC programs actually do? What explains their goals and activities?

The sections of this chapter which follow provide a context for the questions investigated in this book. It begins by examining the philosophical underpinnings and policy consequences of providing legal representation to the poor. Subsequent sections place the questions investigated in this book in historical perspective and outline the study's major purposes. A final section describes the organization of the rest of the book.

EQUALITY, JUDICIAL POLICY, AND LEGAL REPRESENTATION

Legal representation for the poor is a fundamental issue, given its importance for American beliefs regarding the legal and political systems and its crucial influence on judicial policy decisions. Many of our perceptions about the political and legal system are guided by what Stuart Scheingold refers to as "the myth of rights."[6] This complex set of ideals and perceptions is based on a view that political and legal branches of government are related to one another in some respects, but are distinct in others. They are related in the belief that politics and political branches should be governed by "rights and obligations established under law"; rights and obligations pronounced by the legal system.[7] But they are distinct in the functions they perform for society and the roles they play in governing. Political branches, for example, are not expected to consistently respect rights established under law because they respond to popular demands. According to the myth of rights, it is the legal system's role to protect these rights. In short, while political branches represent majority opinion without always considering individual legal rights, courts function to assure a social order that is fair and just by permitting individuals to obtain declarations of rights and force their implementation.[8]

A crucial corollary to this belief system is the normative acceptance of formal legal equality—the ideal that all people regardless of wealth, rank, or privilege should be treated equally before the law and enjoy access to legal institutions. Accepting this ideal is crucial because only by treating all equally and providing equal access may the various rules and rights be applied consistently and nonarbitrarily. Empirical studies suggest some differences based on class and race in Americans' beliefs regarding the legal system's conformity to this ideal,[9] but it is safe to conclude that most Americans treat formal legal equality as both a worthy ideal and an empirical truth describing the actual operations of legal institutions.

The ideal of formal legal equality has influenced the American legal system's development, but the degree of influence may be exaggerated in the popular mind.[10] Its contribution is seen most clearly in one provision of the U.S. Constitution's Sixth Amendment, conferring a right to legal counsel to all citizens charged with a criminal offense. While this provision has been an important source of legal ammunition for several generations of reformers concerned about the legal problems of the poor, it was not established initially to provide the poor with lawyers they could not afford. Instead, the right to counsel originally meant that government could not deny counsel to anyone who could afford it.[11] Thus, the ideal of formal legal equality has played an important symbolic role in American law and politics, but it has not been a consistent empirical feature of the legal system. Indeed, it was not until the 1960s that American government officials took affirmative steps to bridge the gap between myth and reality through the sponsorship of legal programs for the poor.[12]

What difference did it make that legal advocates were not provided the poor for so many years? The unequal distribution of legal services had significant policy consequences—consequences evidenced throughout American history. For example, judicial policy in the formative years of the American Republic sought primarily to protect private property.[13] In the early 1900s, judicial policy served to promote the development of large business and industrial corporations.[14] During these periods, judicial decisions were at best inattentive to the interests of the poor and at worst harmful to them.[15]

One important reason for this bias was the poor's lack of access to the legal system. Without legal advocates the poor could not raise issues of importance to them; nor could they argue against policies advocated by those with resources to use the system. One legal historian writing about the early Supreme Court's bias toward property interests assessed the relationship between legal representation and judicial policy as follows:

> For the kind of social, economic, and political issues that come before the Court depend on the availability of lawyers to various groups and individuals in society. And those with money and power have generally monopolized

the legal profession and through it have had special access to judicial power. The American Civil Liberties Union and the National Association for the Advancement of Colored People have given the poor and anonymous a new voice. But in the days of Marshall and Taney interest group litigation was still limited to privileged groups like the New England Mississippi Land Company or the privately controlled Second Bank of the United States, and thus did not alter the private and exclusivist tendencies of the judicial process.[16]

Spurred by the United States Supreme Court, government officials in the 1960s sought a partial remedy for this inequality. In response to the Supreme Court's decision in *Gideon v. Wainwright,* 372 US 355 (1963), government-sponsored public defender offices opened throughout the country to provide legal assistance to state felony defendants unable to afford an attorney. The Office of Equal Opportunity's (OEO) Legal Services Program was established to provide civil legal services to the poor. These programs offered legal assistance to indigents in volume and scope unprecedented in American history.

Lawyer organizations created at this time sought, among other things, to remedy the policy bias of the legal system against the poor. A variety of techniques and strategies, including test cases brought to appellate courts, class action litigation, and lobbying have been employed to promote the interests of the poor. These strategies produced several successes and contributed to what one observer refers to as the "judicial equality explosion."[17]

This book investigates the operations of one government-financed organization created to provide legal representation for the poor— the Legal Services Program (LSP) and its successor organization, the Legal Services Corporation(LSC). Operating in the civil law area, it has contributed to the "judicial equality explosion" by arguing successfully several important cases.[18] Legal services lawyers have also represented several million indigents in routine legal matters.[19]

A BRIEF HISTORY OF LEGAL ASSISTANCE PROGRAMS

Prior to the 1960s, privately financed legal aid societies offered civil legal assistance for the poor.[20] The legal aid movement may be traced to New York in 1876, when the German Legal Aid Society

(*Der Deutsche Rechtsschutz Verein*) was established to represent German immigrants who could not afford an attorney. The Chicago Women's Club in 1886 established the Protective Agency for Women and Children to provide assistance to these groups. Two years later, the Ethical Culture Society of Chicago organized the first legal aid office to service indigents of all groups.

Legal aid programs grew slowly in the early 1900s, with only 41 organizations established by 1916.[21] The legal aid movement did not grow significantly until the publication of Reginald Heber Smith's influential book, *Justice and the Poor.*[22] Smith's book exposed for the first time the lack of representation for the poor in the American legal system. He argued for the establishment of a national association of legal aid offices to remedy the problem.

Many in the legal profession reacted negatively or with indifference to Smith's book, but some leaders of the American Bar Association were concerned with the book's findings. In response, the ABA devoted its 1920 annual meeting exclusively to discussions of problems in representing the poor. It formed a special committee to deal with the subject, a committee which subsequently became a permanent fixture. In 1923, the National Association of Legal Aid Organizations was established and bar associations throughout the country formed committees to deal with problems in representing the poor in their communities.

Spurred by Smith's book and the legal community's actions, the legal aid movement showed modest growth in the 1920s. Emery Brownell notes that 30 new legal aid offices opened and funds grew substantially.[23] But as the Depression unfolded in America, funds for legal aid dwindled—precisely at a time when legal aid offices represented more clients than ever before in their history.[24]

In the 1930s, the National Lawyers Guild sponsored neighborhood law offices for people of low and moderate incomes in Chicago and Philadelphia and, together with other groups, called for the establishment of a national, federally-funded program.[25] While the ABA had demonstrated some concern for the plight of the poor, it strongly opposed federal funding for legal aid until the 1960s. Indeed, in the 1950s the ABA publicly condemned the idea of federal funding, charging in one resolution it passed that government funding posed a "threat to individual freedom implicit in growing efforts to socialize the legal profession." And a former president of the ABA argued at this time that "the greatest threat aside from the undermining influence of Communist infiltration is the propaganda campaign for a federal subsidy to finance a nationwide plan for legal aid and low cost legal services."[26]

The private legal aid movement did not regain its momentum until the 1950s. During this decade, legal aid experienced rapid growth, increasing its coverage of large cities by 22 percent.[27] Earl Johnson, Jr., attributes this growth to the American bar's response to Great Britain's publicly-funded Legal Aid and Advice program.[28] Fearing the creation of a similar government program, many local bar associations established their own organizations.

According to most observers, several intractable problems beset the legal aid movement. First, being severely underfinanced, legal aid offices could meet only a small portion of the legal needs of the poor.[29] Lawyers typically represented clients on an *ad hoc*, case by case basis, viewing legal problems as specific to individuals rather than as endemic to an underprivileged class.[30] Further, legal aid offices often accepted social values leading to the exclusion of entire case categories, such as divorce, considered inappropriate for the poor.[31] Moreover, these organizations developed close ties to their major funding sources, the local bar association and business establishments, which constrained the types of services provided and clients served.[32]

A movement to provide government-funded legal services to the poor began in the early 1960s. As part of the Johnson Administration's "War on Poverty," a new agency, the Office of Economic Opportunity, was created and given responsibility for operating and coordinating many of the antipoverty programs.[33] By 1965, Congress channeled funds through the OEO for indigent legal assistance.[34] A year later, in the amendments to the Economic Opportunity Act, Congress established the OEO Legal Services Program statutorily.[35]

The Legal Services Program differed in several significant respects from legal aid societies.[36] First, the LSP allocated federal funds for indigent legal services. Storefront law offices opened in the communities' poverty ridden neighborhoods. Community residents selected some members of the program's governing board of directors. Perhaps most important, the LSP emphasized the goal of employing the legal system to reform laws and practices perceived as biased against the poor.[37] "Law reform," as it came to be known, involved legislative and administrative lobbying as well as test cases in appellate courts. Further, legal services programs assisted poor communities in developing their own political and economic resources by helping the poor to organize as groups and advising newly created and extant poverty organizations.

Between 1965 and 1972, LSP lawyers brought many social reform cases.[38] These actions generated a great deal of controversy and opposition from a variety of political, economic, and legal elites. Most of the opposition at the national level came in response to poverty lawyers' law reform activity, particularly successful lawsuits against government agencies. Three times, in 1967, 1969, and 1972, amendments proposed in the United States Senate sought to curtail the program's activities. In 1967, for example, California Senator George Murphy introduced an amendment to bar legal services lawyers from suing any government agency.[39] According to those who have written on the early LSP experience, this amendment came in response to California Rural Legal Assistance's activity, which included legal challenges to cuts in California's Medi-Cal program, and to policies of the United States Department of Labor regarding the importation of alien farm laborers into the state.[40]

At state and local levels, a variety of actors expressed opposition to LSP activity. California Governor Ronald Reagan, along with the governors of Arizona, Connecticut, Florida, and Missouri, vetoed legal services program refundings.[41] The University of Mississippi expelled its OEO-sponsored legal services agency. Community chests, which contributed financial resources to match federal funds in some areas, withdrew their support in St. Louis, Albuquerque, New Orleans, and other cities.[42] In Philadelphia, police commissioner Frank Rizzo announced that department personnel would refrain from contributing to the Community Chest due to its support for a legal services program that brought several lawsuits against the department. Similarly, a Los Angeles police chief denied the University of Southern California access to a municipal communications center because of its cosponsorship of a law reform unit in the area.[43]

Political pressures intensified in the early 1970s when President Richard Nixon appointed Howard Phillips, a political aide, to dismantle OEO.[44] In the face of this challenge, the American Bar Association and other groups in sympathy with LSP goals lobbied hard for a permanent legal services organization removed from the executive branch. After a bitter legislative struggle lasting over three years, President Nixon, who had shifted position on the issue, signed the Legal Services Corporation Act on July 25, 1974.[45]

The Act was intended to cure two major deficiencies in the OEO program.[46] First, it insulated the program from political interference by establishing a quasi-governmental agency controlled by a nonpartisan board of directors. It also prevented programs from using funds and personnel for political purposes by prohibiting organizing activity and lawyer participation in picketing, strikes, and other forms of direct action.[47]

The Legal Services Corporation funds, regulates, and monitors local organizations of lawyers. It is governed by an eleven-member board of directors, a president selected by the board, and an administrative staff. Its major functions are processing grants to local agencies, issuing regulations regarding such things as client eligibility requirements, composition of local governing boards, and client complaint procedures, and auditing and evaluating local program performance. The Corporation also provides technical support, such as training and research, to local grantees.[48]

Between 1975 and 1981, LSC funding grew rapidly from $90 million to $321 million.[49] Further, it expanded its operations from large cities in the North and Far West to cover most of the nation by 1980.[50] As of 1981, 323 local agencies employing approximately 6,200 attorneys and 3,000 paralegals had received funding from the LSC.[51] These agencies served more than one million indigent clients per year.[52]

Prosperity and growth were not the only distinguishing features of the late 1970s for the Corporation. Equally important, its political environment was relatively calm. It seemed to many observers that the creation of a quasi-public corporation had met its goal of shielding the program from political attack. Not only had public opposition to legal services subsided at the national level, but local opposition also appeared to dissipate.[53]

The virtual disappearance of visible opposition to legal services programs led some on the political left to raise questions about the LSC's effectiveness. Left critics asserted that the social reform orientation of legal services programs had become mere rhetoric and charged that poverty lawyers failed to aggressively challenge existing social and political arrangements. Rather than employing the legal system to effect substantive changes in the lives of their clients, legal services programs provided little more than legal "band-aids" for the poor. According to this view, poverty law offices had become overly bureaucratized, responding to heavy caseloads and enormous legal needs by routinely and expeditiously processing clients and cases.[54]

The relative serenity of the late 1970s came to an abrupt end with Ronald Reagan's election in 1980. Howard Phillips, director of the Conservative Caucus and longtime foe of the Corporation, launched an organized effort to abolish it. In a letter to members of Congress and individual supporters, Phillips characterized LSC attorneys as "liberal activists . . . committed to the implementation of a radical social and political agenda." Claiming that some LSC agencies hired "avowed Marxists," he stated that "one big reason for liberal victories and conservative defeats is the Legal Services Corporation."[55]

Reports by the Heritage Foundation[56] and a Reagan transition team[57] also sharply criticized the LSC and served as a justification for the new administration's 1982 budget proposal to terminate it. As one observer notes, these reports questioned the motivations of LSC lawyers and the ultimate result of their activities: "The image conveyed is of a program composed of left-wing lawyers, recently graduated from law school, engaged as self-appointed representatives of the poor in test cases and class actions designed to erode the free enterprise system and to establish a more complete welfare state."[58]

As alternatives to the full-time staff attorney program provided by the LSC, the Reagan administration advocated a greater reliance on *pro bono* legal assistance and judicare programs funded by federal block grants.[59] Consistent with its desire to shift federal responsibilities to state and local governments, judicare programs would be designed and administered by state governments, with little if any federal direction. Both alternatives seek to shift the responsibility for indigents' legal representation from salaried poverty law specialists to local private attorneys.

Because an active coalition supporting the LSC prevented its abolition, the Reagan administration employed other strategies in attempting to bring about its "slow, painful death."[60] By 1984, the LSC's budget had been cut from $321 million to $241 million.[61] Clients were turned away from legal services offices and some offices closed altogether.[62] National board members and administrative staff with little or no poverty law experience and no sympathy for the program's goals were nominated.[63] Thus, the Reagan administration sought to strangle the activity of local agencies by decreasing their resources and appointing national board members who are able to promulgate regulations curtailing the work of attorneys.

PURPOSES OF THIS STUDY

Despite the controversy that has surrounded the Legal Services Corporation and the sharp criticisms aimed at its lawyers by many conservatives and some on the left, little is actually known about the operations of local agencies and the activities of LSC attorneys. While conservatives and those on the left differ dramatically in their descriptions and explanations of LSC activity, few empirical studies systematically examine these questions. What types of activity do local programs actually pursue? Do programs vary in the amount of social reform activity they undertake? What explains the decisions made by LSC programs regarding how to allocate scarce resources in representing the poor?

These questions are investigated in this book through an in-depth examination of five local LSC programs. It will describe the activity of LSC lawyers and assess the effect of three sets of variables: lawyer characteristics (e.g., background, ambition, attitudes, ideology), organizational features (e.g., structure, size, policies), and aspects of the program's environment (e.g., program interactions with external organizations). Theoretical concepts employed in previous research on legal services programs and insights provided by organizational theory are used to develop an integrated model of program activity.

This book also explores the validity of commonly articulated criticisms of the LSC. Is the program composed of "liberal activists" committed to a radical social and political agenda, as conservatives claim? Are the activities of these lawyers guided by their leftist political ideology? Do legal services lawyers routinely process cases, avoiding complex time-consuming social reform activity, as left critics charge? To address these questions, this book describes and analyzes the attitudes and ideological makeup of legal services program personnel, the motivations of LSC lawyers for practicing poverty law, and the activities they pursue.

More generally, this research seeks to contribute to our understanding of the political role of the legal system by answering fundamental questions of concern to legal scholars, social scientists, legal practitioners, and court consumers. To what extent may the legal system be utilized to effect social reform? Under what conditions will lawyers bring legal actions against powerful interests? What political obstacles limit the amount of social reform activity pursued by attorneys?

ORGANIZATION OF THIS WORK

The following chapter introduces the theoretical perspectives employed in this study. It operationally defines the focus of the study—legal services program activity—and discusses possible relationships between activity and lawyer characteristics, aspects of organizational structure and operations, and program environment. Possible interactions between elements of the three perspectives are also explored.

The perspectives presented in Chapter 2 provide a framework for answering the questions raised in this book. They offer a means of describing and explaining the operations of local LSC programs and the activity of their lawyers. Chapter 3 describes the administrative structure of legal services programs, salient features of the local programs selected for study, and some general findings regarding program activity. To provide the reader with a systematic picture of the operations of legal services programs, Chapters 4 and 5 describe in detail two agencies, a medium-sized suburban agency and a much larger metropolitan program that engage in very different mixes of activity. Chapters 6, 7, and 8 explore the utility of the three perspectives in explaining variation in activity among the five programs. Lawyer characteristics are assessed in Chapter 6. Chapter 7 examines organizational features, and Chapter 8 looks at the influence on activity of program environment, as well as assessing explicitly the interactions between personal, organizational, and environmental factors. The final chapter summarizes the politics of delivering legal services to the poor, offers some thoughts on why politics pervade the operations of legal services programs, and considers the impact on the poor of different mixes of legal activity. It concludes with an examination of various proposals for reform. The methodology employed in the research is described and illustrative research instruments are reproduced in appendixes to the book.

NOTES

1. This quote appears in Warren George, "Development of the Legal Services Corporation," *Cornell Law Review* 61 (1976): p. 685.

2. Spiro Agnew, "What's Wrong with the Legal Services Program," *American Bar Association Journal* 58 (1972): p. 931.

3. Stephen Wermiel, "Government-Paid Legal Services for the Poor Stir Local Contention and Growing National Debate," *Wall Street Journal*, June 12, 1981. Quoted in Anthony Champagne, "Legal Services: A Program in Need of Assistance," in Anthony Champagne and Edward J. Harpham, *The Attack on the Welfare State* (Prospect Heights, Illinois: Waveland Press Inc., 1984), p. 143.

4. This quote appears in Roger C. Cramton, "Crisis in Legal Services for the Poor," *Villanova Law Review* 26 (1981): p. 531.

5. There is a substantial literature on these controversies. Among the best works are Harry Stumpf, *Community Politics and Legal Services* (Beverly Hills, California: Sage Publications, 1975); Warren George, "Development of the Legal Services Corporation," *Cornell Law Review* 61 (1976): pp. 681–730; Phillip J. Hannon, "The Murphy Amendments and the Response of the Bar: An Accurate Test of Political Strength," *NLADA Briefcase* (April 1970): pp. 163–169, and "From Politics to Reality: An Historical Perspective of the Legal Services Corporation," *Emory Law Journal* 25 (Summer 1976): pp. 639–654; Walter Karabian, "Legal Services for the Poor: Some Political Observations," *University of San Francisco Law Review* 6 (April 1972): pp. 253–265; Note, "The Legal Services Corporation: Curtailing Political Interference," *Yale Law Journal* 81 (1971): pp. 231–286; Lawrence A. Sullivan, "Law Reform and the Legal Services Crisis," *California Law Review* 59 (1971): pp. 1–28; and Jerome B. Falk and Stuart R. Pollack, "Political Interference with Public Lawyers: The CRLA Controversy and the Future of Legal Services," *Hastings Law Journal* 24 (March 1973): pp. 599–646.

6. Stuart A. Scheingold, *The Politics of Rights: Lawyers, Public Policy, and Political Change* (New Haven, Connecticut: Yale University Press, 1974), chapters 2–3.

7. Ibid., p. 13.

8. Ibid., p. 14.

9. After reviewing the literature, Scheingold concludes that blacks and other minorities are less likely to believe that all are treated as equals by the legal system. See Scheingold, *The Politics of Rights*, chapter 5.

10. For a discussion of the philosophical origins of the notion of formal legal equality and its influence on western legal systems, see Mauro Cappelletti, James Gordley, and Earl Johnson, Jr., *Toward Equal Justice: A Comparative Study of Legal Aid in Modern Societies* (Dobbs Ferry, New York:

Oceana Publications, Inc., 1975), pp. 5–76. Also, see Leon Radzinowitz, *Ideology and Crime* (New York: Columbia University Press, 1966), pp. 1–6.

11. David Fellman, *The Defendant's Rights Today* (Madison, Wisconsin: The University of Wisconsin Press, 1976), p. 211.

12. A good, concise history of public and private efforts to provide legal representation to the poor is Joel F. Handler, Betsy Ginsberg, and Arthur Snow, "The Public Interest Law Industry," in *Public Interest Law: An Economic and Institutional Analysis*, eds. Burton A. Weisbrod, Joel F. Handler, and Neil K. Komesar (Berkeley, California: University of California Press, 1978), pp. 42–79.

13. On this point, see James Willard Hurst, *Law and the Conditions of Freedom in the Nineteenth-Century United States* (Madison, Wisconsin: The University of Wisconsin Press, 1956). Also, see Max Lerner, "The Supreme Court and American Capitalism," in *Essays in Constitutional Law*, ed. Robert G. McCloskey (New York: Alfred A. Knopf, 1957), pp. 107–147.

14. See Arthur Selwyn Miller, *The Supreme Court and American Capitalism* (New York: The Free Press, 1968).

15. See Hurst, *Law and the Conditions of Freedom*, pp. 3–32.

16. R. Kent Newmyer, *The Supreme Court Under Marshall and Taney* (Arlington Heights, Illinois: AHM Publishing Corporation, 1968), pp. 7–8.

17. Frank I. Michelman, "Foreword: On Protecting the Poor Through the Fourteenth Amendment," *Harvard Law Review* 83 (1970): p. 9.

18. For example, *Shapiro v. Thompson*, 394 US 618 (1969), ruled that the residency requirement for welfare recipients was an impermissable purpose under equal protection theory and violated the right of the poor to travel. For other examples of precedent-setting cases brought by legal services programs, see Earl Johnson, Jr., *Justice and Reform: The Formative Years of the American Legal Services Program* (New Brunswick, New Jersey: Transaction Books, 1978).

19. In 1981, for example, legal services lawyers represented over 1.5 million clients. See Legal Services Corporation, *Annual Report* (1981): p. 18.

20. The most comprehensive history of legal aid is Emery Brownell, *Legal Aid in the United States* (Rochester, New York: Lawyers Cooperative Publishing Co., 1951) and *Supplement* (Rochester, New York: Lawyers Cooperative Publishing Co., 1961). Also, see Earl Johnson, Jr., *Justice and Reform*, pp. 5–19. For a critical review of the legal profession's concern for the poor, see Jerold S. Auerbach, *Unequal Justice: Lawyers and Social Change in Modern America* (New York: Oxford University Press, 1976).

21. Carl Patrick McCarthy, "The Consequences of Legal Advocacy:

OEO's Lawyers and the Poor" (unpublished Ph.D. dissertation, University of California, Berkeley, 1974), p. 5.

22. Reginald Heber Smith, *Justice and the Poor* (New York: Carnegie Foundation, 1919).

23. Brownell, *Legal Aid in the United States*, p. 27.

24. Ibid., p. 168.

25. For discussions of efforts by the National Lawyers Guild to represent the poor and their use of neighborhood law offices, see Auerbach, *Unequal Justice*, pp. 203–210, and Alan W. Houseman, "Legal Services and Equal Justice for the Poor: Some Thoughts on Our Future," *NLADA Briefcase* 35 (March 1978): pp. 44–46.

26. Both quotes are taken from Houseman, "Legal Services and Equal Justice," p. 45.

27. Brownell, *Supplement*, p. 68.

28. Johnson, *Justice and Reform*, p. 9.

29. Ibid., p. 9.

30. See Jerome E. Carlin and Jan Howard, "Legal Representation and Class Justice," *UCLA Law Review* 12 (1965): pp. 408–418.

31. Ibid., pp. 413–418.

32. Ibid., pp. 408–413.

33. For a legislative history, see Daniel Patrick Moynihan, *Maximum Feasible Misunderstanding* (New York: The Free Press, 1969). Also of value is John C. Donovan, *The Politics of Poverty* (New York: Pegasus, 1967).

34. The most comprehensive history of the early Legal Services Program is Earl Johnson, Jr., *Justice and Reform*. Also, see Richard Pious, "Congress, the Organized Bar, and the Legal Services Program," *Wisconsin Law Review* (1972): pp. 418–446.

35. Section 211–1 (b), Economic Opportunity Amendments of 1966, Public Law 89–794, November 8, 1966, 80 Stat. 1472.

36. Several articles discuss the goals and structure of the Legal Services Program. Perhaps the most influential at the time of program origin was Edgar S. Cahn and Jean C. Cahn, "The War on Poverty: A Civilian Perspective," *Yale Law Journal* 73 (July 1964): pp. 1317–1352. Other useful articles are A. Kenneth Pye, "The Role of Legal Services in the Anti-Poverty Program," *Law and Contemporary Problems* 31 (Winter 1966): pp. 211–249; and Note, "Neighborhood Law Offices: The New Wave in Legal Services for the Poor," *Harvard Law Review* 80 (February 1967): pp. 805–850.

37. Johnson, *Justice and Reform*, pp. 132–134.

38. See Johnson, *Justice and Reform*, pp. 187–234; and Anthony Champagne, "An Evaluation of the Effectiveness of the OEO Legal Services Program," *Urban Affairs Quarterly* 9 (June 1974): pp. 465–489. For a view that the LSP did not engage in a large amount of law reform activity, see

Richard Pious, "Policy and Public Administration: The Legal Services Program in the War on Poverty," *Politics and Society* 1 (May 1971): pp. 365–391.

39. 13 *Congressional Record*, pt. 21, at page 27871.

40. See Falk and Pollack, "Political Interference," and John R. Robb, "Controversial Cases and the Legal Services Program," *American Bar Association Journal* 56 (April 1970): pp. 329–331.

41. Johnson, *Justice and Reform*, p. 193.

42. Stumpf, *Community Politics*, p. 256–258.

43. Johnson, *Justice and Reform*, p. 193.

44. On the LSP during the Nixon years, see Johnson, "Forword to the New Edition," in *Justice and Reform*, pp. ix-xxvii; Note, "The Legal Services Corporation: Curtailing Political Interference," pp. 231–259; and Cramton, "Crisis in Legal Services for the Poor," pp. 522–528.

45. 120 *Congressional Record*, at page H7371, 1974. For a discussion of the legislative struggle, see the sources in note 44 plus Warren George, "Development," pp. 681–730; Mark Arnold, "The Knockdown, Drag-Out Battle Over Legal Services," *Juris Doctor* (April 1973): pp. 4–10; "The Odyssey of Legal Services and the Games Politicians Play," *Juris Doctor* (October 1974): pp. 23–28, and "And Finally, 342 Days Later," *Juris Doctor* (September 1975): pp. 32–38.

46. See Cramton, "Crisis in Legal Services for the Poor," p. 526.

47. Constitutional questions raised by these prohibitions are discussed in Note, "Depoliticizing Legal Aid: A Constitutional Analysis of the Legal Services Corporation Act," *Cornell Law Review* 61 (1976): pp. 734–776.

48. Cramton, "Crisis in Legal Services for the Poor," p. 529.

49. Champagne, "Legal Services: A Program in Need of Assistance," p. 142.

50. Legal Services Corporation, *Annual Report* (1981): p. 7.

51. Ibid., pp. 8–9.

52. Ibid., p. 18.

53. See Gary Bellow, "Turning Solutions into Problems: The Legal Aid Experience," *NLADA Briefcase* (August 1977): pp. 106–107.

54. These views are discussed in Gary Bellow, "Turning Solutions Into Problems."

55. Letter from National Defeat Legal Services Committee to Congressman Robert F. Drinan, September 8, 1980. This letter was circulated by the National Legal Aid and Defender Association to warn of trouble ahead for the LSC. Letter in author's files. For a similar statement, see Howard Phillips, "Legal Services Should Not be Federally Funded," *Conservative Digest* (July 1980): pp. 31–32.

56. Heritage Foundation, *Mandate for Leadership: Project Team Report on the Poverty Agencies* (October 22, 1980).

57. For a description of this study, see Cramton, "Crisis in Legal Services for the Poor," p. 522.

58. Ibid., p. 521.

59. Champagne, "Legal Services: A Program in Need of Assistance," pp. 142–143.

60. This phrase is used by Cramton, "Crisis in Legal Services for the Poor," p. 521.

61. Champagne, "Legal Services: A Program in Need of Assistance," pp. 142–143.

62. Ibid., p. 143.

63. Ibid., pp. 143–144.

2

TOWARD A THEORY OF LEGAL ACTIVITY

Since the creation of the Legal Services Corporation in 1974, only a few researchers have examined the questions raised in this study.[1] However, during the late 1960s and early 1970s, when OEO administered the program, the issue of legal services program activity was explored more extensively.[2]

While research on the OEO program is suggestive, its findings can not be applied with confidence to local LSC programs. For one thing, differences in goals and funding mechanisms make it difficult to apply earlier research findings to the present program. During its formative years, the OEO pronounced law reform as its major goal.[3] To encourage local grantees to engage in social reform activity, national OEO officials allocated funding to local programs based on the amount of law reform pursued.[4] In sharp contrast, the LSC has avoided stating explicit program goals and allocates funds to local grantees by formula, based on the number of people in the program's service area living below the Office of Management and Budget's (OMB) poverty line. Thus, while national OEO officials may have exerted influence on local grantees through its explicit statement of goals and method of funding, LSC officials are unable to do so.

The geographic scope of the OEO program and the LSC also differs significantly. OEO-funded programs were located primarily in large metropolitan settings. The LSC expanded its coverage to rural America throughout the 1970s.[5]

Despite the attention researchers paid to the OEO program, few offered theoretical advances. Most of the research is descriptive or guided by narrow, undeveloped theory. Several of these studies rely solely on impressionistic measures of activity. Thus, while previous research findings are important preliminary steps in theory building, they do not provide a sophisticated or systematic picture of how legal services agencies operate or why they differ in activity.[6] To better understand program differences, this study uses insights from previous research, elaborates a more systematic framework, and borrows from recent work in organizational theory.

In this chapter, three perspectives suggested either explicitly or implicitly by previous research are developed and discussed. The first derives from previous work that explores relationships between staff characteristics and lawyer activity. A second perspective borrows from both previous research on legal services and organizational theory, assessing the relationship between organizational features, such as structure, policies, and procedures, and program activity. A third perspective derives from work on interorganizational theory, exploring the influence on activity mixes of legal services program interaction with other organizations (e.g., bar associations, judiciary, community organizations).

The following section of this chapter defines and discusses the central focus of this study—the activities pursued by legal services programs. Subsequent sections elaborate the individual-level, organizational, and interorganizational perspectives. A final section explores possible interactions between elements of the three perspectives as an initial step in developing an integrated model.

THE ACTIVITIES OF LEGAL SERVICES AGENCIES

Resource constraints prevent legal services programs from handling all legal problems brought to them by the eligible poor.[7] Choices must be made regarding the types of cases to handle and strategies to employ in disposing of them. Two basic categories of activities are referred to throughout this book. Those actions aimed at solving the problems of individual clients are labeled "service" activities, while those intended to benefit large numbers of the poor are "reform" oriented. The informal negotiation of a landlord-tenant problem, for example, typically is intended to benefit an individual client or small set of clients and thus is considered a service activity.

Attempts to change existing laws through appeals to higher courts or the filing of class action suits are reform activities, for they seek to benefit a poverty class.

Regardless of whether lawyers engage in service or reform activity, two conceptually distinct processes are involved. The first is referred to by Donald J. Black as the "mobilization of legal issues," the manner in which legal issues arise.[8] Lawyers may wait reactively for individuals to define problems or proactively search for problems and clients to serve a particular class interest.[9] In practice, legal services programs are not expected to employ one process exclusively, but rather to emphasize one method of mobilization over the other to varying degrees. The second process involves the lawyer's choice of a strategy for problem resolution. Four strategies are available to legal services lawyers—informal negotiation, *ad hoc* litigation, law reform, and legislative and administrative advocacy.

Informal negotiation involves bargaining with an opposing party to settle a dispute without formally invoking the legal system. For example, a lawyer may call a client's landlord and negotiate a week's extension for a rental payment or meet with a creditor to discuss a satisfactory payment schedule.

Alternatively, an attorney may litigate issues on an *ad hoc* basis. This strategy is invoked when a lawyer brings problems unresolved by negotiations to a local trial court with the intention of resolving an individual's problem.

Law reform or impact litigation is a strategy that seeks to win legal victories for a large segment of the poverty community through the institution of class action procedures or appeals of lower court decisions on broad principles of law. One observer explains, "the few clients directly represented in these cases are said to be only a legal sample of large numbers who are similarly situated."[10] Finally, lawyers may choose legislative or administrative fora for problem resolution. Attorneys acting on behalf of low-income groups or individuals lobby for legislation and regulations beneficial to the poor or against those which harm them.

As Table 1 depicts, mobilization and choice of strategy interact. Proactive lawyers who identify broad policy problems affecting clients tend to rely on law reform and advocacy through lobbying. Reactive lawyers less often identify broad policy problems, and as Leon H. Mayhew hypothesizes, tend to service "the clients' interests

Table 1
Mobilization Process by Strategy of Representation

Strategy	Mobilization Process Proactive	Reactive
Law Reform	x	
Lobbying	x	
Informal Negotiation		x
Ad Hoc Litigation		x

as clients perceive them," utilizing "compromise, minimum delay and expense, and taking what one can."[11]

STAFF CHARACTERISTICS AND PROGRAM ACTIVITY

One general perspective derived from literature on the OEO program posits that program behavior is shaped primarily by the characteristics of program personnel, including attitudes, values, and ideologies. Anthony Champagne, for example, using data on over 200 local programs collected by the Auerbach and Kettelle Corporations, concluded that individual characteristics of program decisionmakers and staff lawyers are more important for explaining differences in program "effectiveness" in law reform, case-handling, and community development, than the demographic makeup of client communities, budgetary levels, caseloads, or group pressures.[12] Ted Finman reported a relationship between the ideology of agency initiators and managers and the pursuit of social reform in five local programs he studied. According to Finman, "whether the program will pursue social change and, if so, whether the goal will have priority over others, depends mainly on the ideology and ideological image that come to the program from the persons and process that bring it into being."[13]

Other studies suggest that lawyers' backgrounds influence program activity. Joel Handler et al. found statistically significant, though weak, relationships between certain aspects of lawyers' backgrounds and their activity.[14] For example, class standing and parents' political orientation and experience seemed to relate to the amount of law reform pursued by individual lawyers. Also, the location of a lawyer's upbringing has been suggested to influence activity. Richard Pious argued that the service orientation of one agency he studied was explained in part by the large number of lawyers born and raised in the local community.[15] He asserted that these attorneys are more likely than "outsiders" to accept local values and practices and, therefore, less likely to challenge established institutions.

Ambitions are another important personal influence on activity suggested by previous research. Jack Katz, for example, found that lawyers in Chicago's Legal Aid Bureau rarely pursued social reform activity in part because they wanted to enter private practice in Chicago, an ambition leading them to develop close relations with the local bar and "accept the way the legal professional environment defined the problems of the poor."[16]

The individual-level perspective is accepted implicitly by conservative critics of the LSC. Most assume a simple relationship between personal characteristics of poverty lawyers, particularly backgrounds, attitudes, and ideologies, and legal activity. The activity of poverty lawyers, it is argued, is shaped primarily by their leftist political values, leading to activity mixes in local programs weighted heavily toward policy suits and lobbying.

However, the individual-level perspective does not necessarily support such a view. Rather than fostering law reform activity, personal characteristics may discourage it. Poverty lawyers with certain personal features, such as more moderate political values or ambitions to practice law privately in the local community, may avoid filing lawsuits seeking social reform.

ORGANIZATIONAL CHARACTERISTICS AND PROGRAM ACTIVITY

Previous literature on OEO programs links several policies and procedures of local agencies to their activity mix. A few authors, for example, view recruitment criteria as important determinants of program activity. Pious, for instance, argued that the service orientation of one program he studied was due in part to the recruitment practices of the program's governing board, a body dominated by members of the local bar association.[17] Local lawyers with close ties to the community and a service orientation to legal work were given preference by the board in hiring decisions. Finman linked the recruitment process to the ideologies of agency initiators and managers, treating recruitment as an intervening variable.[18] Directors of local agencies, he argued, hired staff lawyers with compatible attitudes and predispositions regarding the proper mix of activity. Once hired, they engaged in activities consistent with their predispositions.

Katz argued that evaluation measures employed by agencies affected their activity mix.[19] Evaluations conducted by managers of Chicago's Legal Aid Bureau centered on each lawyer's ability to develop and maintain close working relations with local lawyers and the local judiciary. These criteria provided an incentive for legal aid lawyers to cooperate with the local legal establishment in the processing of cases, relying in large part on informal negotiations and bargaining.

Caseload policies have also been hypothesized to affect activity mixes. Carol Ruth Silver, for example, argued that the lack of program policies limiting the caseloads of staff lawyers results in lawyers choosing by necessity to handle cases in the least time-consuming manner.[20] She writes, "Among the multitude of 'cases' presented by any client the lawyer is limited to taking only those cases that do not require more than a minimum of thought, effort, time, and skill."[21] Thus, the lack of caseload policies may force lawyers to avoid using reform strategies to resolve problems presented in cases with reform potential.

A final organizational practice that may influence a program's activity mix is the nature of training provided new members. Training as a method of inculcating values and shaping behavior is recognized by several organizational theorists.[22] It may be expected that service oriented programs train lawyers to engage in service activity, while reform oriented programs teach new members the mechanics of class action litigation, test case development, and lobbying techniques.

Elements of the organizational perspective are accepted implicitly by left critics of the LSC. They argue that organizational policies and practices do not respond appropriately to enormous demands for service and lead poverty lawyers, regardless of their personal philosophies, to handle all or most cases, even those with reform potential, in routine ways. To keep their heads above water in a vast sea of cases, legal services lawyers develop and apply routinized methods for "sizing-up" and disposing cases, leading to activity mixes virtually devoid of social reform efforts.

Of course, the organizational perspective does not predict that organizational features of local programs necessarily promote individual client service and discourage law reform. Programs with certain characteristics, such as recruitment policies favoring reform oriented lawyers, evaluation criteria emphasizing social reform, training in test case and class action techniques, and caseload limitation policies, will likely engage in at least some legal reform activity.

INTERORGANIZATIONAL RELATIONS AND PROGRAM ACTIVITY

A third perspective is suggested by research on the OEO program examining sources of support and opposition to local agencies. Two suggestive studies report that external organizations exerted some influence on program activity. Harry P. Stumpf, Henry P. Schroerluke, and Forrest D. Dill argued that despite political opposition, the San Francisco Legal Assistance Foundation and California Rural Legal Assistance engaged in reform activity because of support received from liberal groups, such as organized labor.[23] And Stumpf and Robert J. Janowitz found that the actions of lawyers in several California legal services programs were influenced by the attitudes and behavior of local judges.[24] Certain procedural devices, such as *in forma pauperis* petitions, were used rarely and certain types of cases were not pursued before judges openly hostile to them.

These studies suggest that the local agency's context, particularly its relations with outside groups, may influence its mix of service and reform activity. Indeed, the possibility of external influences on local agencies is underscored by the work of Handler et al., who found that 60 percent of the legal services lawyers in their national survey reported receiving pressure from bar groups and private lawyers to engage in less reform work, while 31 percent reported receiving pressure from OEO officials and client groups to engage in more reform work.[25]

To go beyond previous research in assessing the influence of external groups on the work activity of local legal services agencies, a more general theoretical framework is needed. Aspects of organizational theory dealing with interorganizational relations provide such a framework.

James D. Thompson presents a thoughtful treatment of the environment's importance for understanding organizational behavior.[26] He argues that organizations, above all else, seek to survive. In order to survive, they must control relevant environmental segments, referred to as the "task environment," which provide essential inputs. In effect, organizations attempt to regulate the flow of inputs by controlling those actors responsible for them. The effective control of environmental actors serves an important function for the organization, reducing or eliminating uncertainty.

Work by Thompson and William J. McEwen highlights the importance of the survival goal for understanding organizational behavior.[27] They argue that an organization's goals and activity are shaped by the desire to control environmental uncertainty that threatens survival. Some valued activity must be offered to relevant environmental actors in exchange for support. Effective organizations are those able to set goals that satisfy a task environment.

Recently, organizational theorists have focused on the increasing density of organizations in society. As a consequence of increased organizational density, the organizations' task environment has become populated to a much greater extent by other organizations. Recognizing that interaction among organizations has increased, several theorists identify various interaction patterns and assess their impact on behavior.

Sol Levine and Paul E. White, for example, identify "exchange" as a theoretically important interaction between organizations.[28] Exchange relationships result from recognition that both organizations benefit from cooperation. "Domain consensus," agreement on specific organizational goals and functions, is a necessary condition for cooperation.

A second form of exchange occurs when organizations within a network are unequal in power. "Power-dependence" relations are characterized by organizations employing their influence within a network to force linkages with other organizations.[29] According to this perspective, organizations that control critical resources of another organization are considered powerful.[30] Controlling resources enables the powerful organization to shape the dependent organization's activity.

When examining actual relations between organizations, it is often difficult to separate exchange from power-dependence. Stuart M. Schmidt and Thomas A. Kochan argue that organizations are likely to engage in a mixture of exchange and power-dependence interactions.[31] Further, no single relationship is purely one type or the other. Instead, most relationships are products of "mixed motives." In response to this mix, organizations segment relevant environmental actors and adopt unique strategies for dealing with each.

Although organizations typically interact with a wide variety of other organizations, not all are able to shape behavior. Certain organizations are more important to the focal organization than others. Those considered most important compose the focal organization's "enacted environment."[32] An enacted environment does not necessarily refer to an organization's objective setting, but is rather the focal organization's perception of which external groups are most salient. Consequently, the organization's response to environmental demand is conditioned by the external actor's perceived importance. Jeffrey Pfeffer and Gerald R. Salancik argue that organizational effectiveness depends on the organization's ability to rank all organizations within its network and satisfy the demands of those most important objectively for its continued survival.[33]

Interorganizational theory has been applied usefully by others to explain organizational structures and behavior,[34] but most of these empirical studies examine private sector organizations.[35] In applying this perspective to legal services programs—a government funded program—a few modifications are necessary, modifications identified in the discussion that follows.

The variant of the interorganizational perspective applied to this study is referred to by Pfeffer and Salancik as "resource dependence."[36] In general terms, it posits that a local legal services program's mobilization process and choice of strategies is understood best through examination of its interorganizational environment. While previous work in interorganizational theory provides several conceptual schemes for categorizing interorganizational environments, they are not particularly useful for studies employing a resource dependence approach.[37] For purposes of this study, interorganizational environments may vary on four dimensions important for explaining differences in activity mixes. They are (1) the degree of consensus among external organizations regarding appropriate legal services activity, (2) the composition of the enacted environment, (3) critical resources, and (4) the activity preferences of salient external organizations.

Program environments differ in the degree to which external organizations agree about appropriate activities. Monolithic environments only include organizations that prefer service to individual clients and oppose law reform. In such an environment, legal services programs have no choice but to seek critical resources among groups preferring service to law reform.

Alternatively, some environments are pluralistic, including organizations that differ in their preferences. One set encourages service to individual clients, while a second set prefers law reform. In pluralistic environments, programs may choose their major source of critical resources from among groups making competing demands.

Whether the interorganizational environment is monolithic or pluralistic, program policymakers and staff consider as salient only a subset of external groups that potentially may offer critical resources. This subset is referred to as the "enacted environment." Even when faced with the same or similar "objective" environments, legal services programs may attend to different aspects.

External organizations may provide a variety of resources deemed critical by policymakers and staff. Dependency relations are expected to develop between legal services offices and other organizations perceived to control critical resources. Previous research suggests two primary critical resources, money and authority,[38] but because the LSC funds local agencies by means of a nondiscretionary formula, other types of resources must be considered. Resources which may be deemed critical by program personnel fall into several categories.

Consistent with previous work on interorganizational dependency, legal services programs may rely on external organizations for financial resources. The LSC, state government, local funding sources, and organizations that exert influence on the allocation of funds received from other sources (e.g., the governing board of directors), may be viewed as salient for their control of program funding. Important political resources may be controlled by external organizations. Organizations may lobby for continued or increased funding of legal services agencies at the state and national levels. A variety of social resources may be controlled by external actors. For example,

Table 2
Dimensions of the Interorganizational Environment

Dimension	Categories
Degree of Consensus	pluralistic, monolithic
Composition of Enacted Environment	local, state, and national organizations
Critical Resources	financial, political, social, decisional, case processing, career, informational
Activity Preference	reform, service

program personnel may depend on other organizations for approval and respect.

Decisional resources are controlled by judges and opposition attorneys who render judgments affecting clients, and may be deemed critical by program staff. The legal community may also be perceived as controlling important case processing resources, such as assisting legal services lawyers in disposing of cases quickly or representing indigents in cases that the program is unwilling or unable to handle. Further, career resources of importance to program staff may be controlled by judges and the private bar. Members of the legal community may be able to assist legal services lawyers in gaining employment in the private bar.

Finally, external organizations may control information considered critical, which may include data regarding poverty community problems or the identification of prospective plaintiffs for lawsuits.

A fourth important dimension of interorganizational environments is the activity preferences of groups composing the enacted environment. Organizations salient to personnel may prefer and encourage service to individual clients or law reform.

The four dimensions of the interorganizational environment and the manner in which they may vary among programs are depicted in Table 2.

In summary, the resource dependence perspective suggests that legal services program activity depends on the nature of its interactions with external groups. It predicts that proactive, reform oriented programs depend on external groups encouraging the use of legal services resources for social reform. On the other hand, reactive service oriented programs will depend on organizations encouraging a more traditional mobilization process and the use of conventional legal strategies.

The interorganizational perspective suggests that both conservative and left critics of legal services fundamentally misunderstand organizational decisionmaking and behavior. Even if legal services lawyers tend to hold leftist political values, as conservatives argue, their values will not translate into reform legal activity unless they work in programs surrounded by like-minded organizations that provide critical resources, such as political support. Left critics may accurately describe the service activities of programs as mere "band-aids," but the interorganizational perspective suggests that the reliance of programs on external groups preferring such activity, rather than program policies or bureaucratic tendencies, explains it. Therefore, this perspective seriously challenges many of the assumptions underlying criticisms of the LSC offered by individuals with widely divergent political orientations.

TOWARD AN INTERACTIVE MODEL

The three perspectives are not mutually exclusive. While they may contribute independently to an explanation of activity, they also may interact with one another. The process of building an interactive model begins in this section through a discussion of several plausible interactions between elements of the three perspectives.

As Finman suggests in his study of OEO programs, the attitudes of legal services policymakers may affect organizational policies.[39] For example, policymakers holding left of center political attitudes and a reformist orientation toward legal representation may recruit like-minded staff lawyers and enact policies, such as caseload limitations, permitting them to engage in law reform. On the other hand, program policymakers holding conservative, service oriented attitudes may recruit staff with similar predispositions and enact policies requiring them to handle large service caseloads.

Policymaker attitudes may also affect the choice of external organizations composing the enacted environment. Attitudes may determine, at least in part, the resources controlled by external organizations that are deemed "critical." Conservative administrators, for example, may value social resources controlled by the established bar, while more liberal administrators seek the respect of liberal interest groups and low-income advocacy organizations.

The organization's environment may affect its policies. If few organizations in the community favor resource allocations to law reform activity, policymakers may avoid enacting policies that encourage it. If, on the other hand, a large number of organizations favor law reform over service, administrators may respond by excluding a number of case categories, thus permitting lawyers to spend the time necessary to bring broad policy suits.

The interactions just discussed are logical possibilities, but are not grounded in the empirical world. To determine how these variables actually influence activity and interact with one another, structured empirical research is needed. The presentation of findings of this research begins in the next chapter.

NOTES

1. See Carrie Menkel-Meadow and Robert G. Meadow, "Resource Allocation in Legal Services: Individual Attorney Decisions in Work Priorities," *Law and Policy Quarterly* 5 (1983): pp. 237–256. They examined the tasks performed by LSC lawyers in one urban program.

The Legal Services Corporation conducted its own study of local agencies, comparing the performance of LSC funded programs to 38 demonstration projects, including judicare programs, prepaid legal services, organized *pro bono* programs, contracts with private firms, voucher programs, and legal clinics. See *The Delivery Systems Study: A Policy Report to the Congress and President of the United States* (Washington, D.C.: Legal Services Corporation, June 1980).

2. The most noteworthy examples of this voluminous literature are Anthony Champagne, "An Evaluation of the Effectiveness of the OEO Legal Services Program," *Urban Affairs Quarterly* 9 (June 1974): pp. 465–489; "The Internal Operations of OEO Legal Services Projects," *Journal of Urban Law* 51 (1974): pp. 649–664; and *Legal Services: An Exploratory Study of Effectiveness* (Beverly Hills, California: Sage Professional Paper, Administrative and Policy Studies Series, volume 3, 1976): pp. 5–44; Richard Pious, "Policy and Public Administration: The Legal Services Program in the War on Poverty," *Politics and Society* 1 (May 1971): pp. 365–391; Ted Finman, "OEO Legal Services Programs and the Pursuit of Social Change: The

Relationship Between Program Ideology and Program Performance," *Wisconsin Law Review* (1971): pp. 1001–1084; Joel F. Handler, Ellen Jane Hollingsworth, and Howard S. Erlanger, *Lawyers and the Pursuit of Legal Rights* (New York: Academic Press, 1978); Jack Katz, *Poor People's Lawyers in Transition* (New Brunswick, New Jersey: Rutgers University Press, 1982); and Harry Stumpf, *Community Politics and Legal Services* (Beverly Hills, California: Sage Publications, 1975).

3. See Earl Johnson, Jr., *Justice and Reform: The Formative Years of the American Legal Services Program* (New Brunswick, New Jersey: Transaction Books, 1978), chapter 5.

4. Ibid., chapter 7.

5. For a discussion of the urban bias of the OEO program, see Leonard H. Goodman and Margaret H. Walker, *The Legal Services Program: Resource Distribution and the Low Income Population* (Washington, D.C.: Bureau of Social Science Research, Inc., 1975), pp. 57–59. On the geographical expansion of the LSC, see Legal Services Corporation, *Annual Report* (1977), pp. 18–19.

6. For a more detailed critique of research on the OEO program, see Mark Kessler, "The Interorganizational Politics of Legal Services Agencies" (Ph.D. dissertation, Pennsylvania State University, 1985), pp. 33–53. Examples of methodological problems plaguing much of the previous research are discussed in Richard Berk, "Champagne's Assessment of Legal Services Programs: An Evaluation of an Evaluation," *Urban Affairs Quarterly* 9 (June 1974): pp. 490–509.

7. See Carol Ruth Silver, "The Imminent Failure of Legal Services for the Poor: Why and How to Limit Caseloads," *Journal of Urban Law* 46 (1969): pp. 217–248.

8. Donald J. Black, "The Mobilization of Law," *The Journal of Legal Studies* 2 (January 1973): pp. 125–149.

9. See Leon H. Mayhew, "Institutions of Legal Representation: Civil Justice and the Public," *Law and Society Review* 10 (Spring 1975): pp. 401–429.

10. Harry Brill, "The Uses and Abuses of Legal Assistance," *The Public Interest* 31 (Spring 1973): p. 39.

11. Mayhew, "Institutions of Representation," p. 415.

12. See Champagne, *Legal Services*, pp. 5–41.

13. Finman, "OEO Legal Services Programs," p. 1007.

14. See Handler et al., *Lawyers and the Pursuit*, pp. 146–150.

15. Pious, "Policy and Public Administration," pp. 380–381.

16. Katz, *Poor People's Lawyers*, p. 62.

17. Pious, "Policy and Public Administration," p. 380.

18. Finman, "OEO Legal Services Programs," p. 1071.

19. Katz, *Poor People's Lawyers*, p.61.

20. Silver, "The Imminent Failure of Legal Services," pp. 224–227.

21. Ibid., p. 226.

22. See, for example, Herbert Simon, *Administrative Behavior*, 3rd ed. (New York: The Free Press, 1976), pp. 169–171.

23. Harry P. Stumpf, Henry P. Schroerluke, and Forrest D. Dill, "The Legal Profession and Legal Services: Explorations in Local Bar Politics," *Law and Society Review* 6 (August 1971): pp. 47–67.

24. Harry P. Stumpf and Robert J. Janowitz, "Judges and the Poor: Bench Responses to Federally Funded Legal Services," *Stanford Law Review* 21 (1969): pp. 1058–1076.

25. Handler et al., *Lawyers and the Pursuit*, pp. 64–65.

26. James D. Thompson, *Organizations in Action* (New York: McGraw-Hill Book Company, 1967).

27. James D. Thompson and William J. McEwen, "Organizational Goals and Environment: Goal-Setting as an Interaction Process," *American Sociological Review* 23 (1958): pp. 23–31.

28. Sol Levine and Paul E. White, "Exchange as a Conceptual Framework for the Study of Interorganizational Relationships," *Administrative Science Quarterly* 5 (March 1961): pp. 583–601.

29. See J. Kenneth Benson, "The Interorganizational Network as a Political Economy," *Administrative Science Quarterly* 20 (June 1975); pp. 229–248; and Karen S. Cook, "Exchange and Power in Networks of Interorganizational Relations," *Sociological Quarterly* 18 (1977): pp. 62–82.

30. See Jeffrey Pfeffer and Gerald R. Salancik, *The External Control of Organizations* (New York: Harper and Row, 1978).

31. Stuart M. Schmidt and Thomas A. Kochan, "Interorganizational Relationships: Patterns and Motivations," *Administrative Science Quarterly* 22 (June 1977): pp. 220–235.

32. Pfeffer and Salancik, *The External Control of Organizations*, pp. 71–78.

33. Ibid., p. 60.

34. For examples, see Jeffrey Pfeffer, "Merger as a Response to Organizational Interdependence," *Administrative Science Quarterly* 17 (September 1973): pp. 382–392; Jeffrey Pfeffer and Phillip Nowak, "Joint Ventures and Interorganizational Dependence," *Administrative Science Quarterly* 21 (September 1976): pp. 398–418; Burton Clark, "Interorganizational Patterns in Education," *Administrative Science Quarterly* 10 (September 1965): pp. 224–237; Howard E. Aldrich, "Resource Dependence and Interorganizational Relations: Local Employment Service Offices and Social Services Sector Organizations," *Administration and Society* 7 (February 1976): pp. 419–454; Murray Milner, Jr., *Unequal Care: A Case Study of Interorganizational Re-*

lations in Health Care (New York: Columbia University Press, 1980); and Virginia Gray and Bruce A. Williams, *The Organizational Politics of Criminal Justice* (Lexington, Massachusetts: Lexington Books, 1980). For a more comprehensive review of the literature published prior to 1980, see Howard E. Aldrich, *Organizations and Environments* (Englewood Cliffs, New Jersey: Prentice-Hall, 1979).

35. However, a few studies look at public organizations. One of the best studies applies interorganizational theory to the Law Enforcement Assistance Administration. See Virginia Gray and Bruce Williams, *The Organizational Politics of Criminal Justice*.

36. Pfeffer and Salancik, *The External Control of Organizations*, especially chapter 10.

37. Other conceptual schemes are presented in F. E. Emery and E. L. Trist, "The Causal Texture of Organizational Environments," *Human Relations* 18 (February 1965): pp. 21–32; Shirley Terreberry, "The Evolution of Organizational Environments," *Administrative Science Quarterly* 12 (March 1968): pp. 590–613; Cora Bagley Marrett, "On the Specification of Interorganizational Dimensions," *Sociology and Social Research* 56 (1971): pp. 83–99; Robert B. Duncan, "Characteristics of Organizational Environments and Perceived Environmental Uncertainty," *Administrative Science Quarterly* 17 (September 1972): pp. 313–327; Ray Jurkovich, "A Core Typology of Organizational Environments," *Administrative Science Quarterly* 19 (September 1974): pp. 380–394; Richard H. Hall, John P. Clark, Peggy C. Giordano, Paul V. Johnson, and Martha Van Roekel, "Patterns of Interorganizational Relationships," *Administrative Science Quarterly* 22 (September 1977): pp. 457–474; and Howard E. Aldrich, *Organizations and Environments*.

38. See Benson, "The Interorganizational Network as a Political Economy," pp. 229–248; and Gray and Williams, *The Organizational Politics of Criminal Justice*, p.27.

39. Finman, "OEO Legal Services Programs," p. 1071.

3

THE OPERATING ENVIRONMENT OF LEGAL SERVICES PROGRAMS

This chapter examines the operating environment of the five programs selected for study. All of the programs studied are located in a single state. Two of these, Metro City Legal Services (MCLS) and Industrial Region Legal Services (IRLS), are large metropolitan programs; two others, Rustic Legal Services (RLS) and Regional Rural Legal Services (RegRLS), are smaller rural agencies; and one, Suburban Legal Services (SLS), is a medium-sized suburban program.[1]

The discussion begins with a description of the formal administrative structure of legal services programs, focusing on the mechanisms available to state and national officials to influence the activity of local programs. In a subsequent section, salient characteristics of the programs and their local environments are described. A final section completes the introduction to the research sites by examining differences in their mix of activity.

NATIONAL AND STATE ENVIRONMENT

The five programs examined in this book are funded and administered by the national Legal Services Corporation and an analogous state agency. On the national level, the LSC receives all of its funding from the United States Congress. Since the Corporation was established to prevent political officials from interfering with or directing the daily operations of local programs, Congress cannot use its funding to influence particular programs. Instead, federal monies are allocated by Congress to thc LSC to distribute among local agencies.

While Congress is prohibited from using funds to shape local lawyers' behavior, a variety of statutory provisions in the Legal Services Corporation Act and its amendments restrict the discretion of local program personnel. For example, lawyers are prohibited from organizing low-income groups and participating in demonstrations.[2] Lobbying and testifying at public hearings on behalf of the poor are not permitted unless the lawyer is representing a particular client, is invited to appear by a member of the legislature or administrative body, or is appearing in regard to legislation or regulations that affect the funding and operations of the LSC.[3] Further, local program lawyers may not participate in voter registration drives or transport voters to the polls.[4] Legal services lawyers are also prohibited from handling cases in a variety of areas, such as those producing a fee, criminal matters, cases in which a client seeks a nontherapeutic abortion, school desegregation cases, violations of the Selective Service Act, and desertion from the military.[5] Money allocated to the LSC as well as any nonfederal funds obtained by local programs may not be used to handle cases in these areas.[6]

Funds allocated by Congress to the LSC are administered by a national governing board and a full-time administrative staff. In contrast to the national leadership of the OEO Legal Services Program, LSC officials have not used funding as a resource for influencing the mix of activities at the local level. Funds are allocated to programs by formula based on the number of people in the community served with incomes below the poverty line.

The LSC's governing board, however, does promulgate regulations for local programs. They cover such areas as client eligibility, client complaint procedures, and the composition of local governing boards. At the time of my research, the national board had not issued regulations restricting legal activity at the local level beyond that which is stated explicitly in the legislation.[7]

The state in which the five programs are located also allocates a significant amount of funding to them. In 1981, for example, the state appropriated $3 million to legal services as part of a match of federal Social Security Act, Title XX monies for social services. State matched Title XX funds constitute a significant portion of local program budgets, ranging from 40 to 60 percent of the total.

The state's funding process is complex and involves several agencies. The state's Department of Welfare (DOW) begins the process by submitting a federally mandated social services plan to the legislature. The plan describes the types of programs to be funded and the anticipated distribution of funds among programs. The state legislature uses the plan as a guide, but may make any changes it desires. The legislature, then, may fund a particular program, such as day care or legal services, at higher or lower levels than is suggested by the DOW or it may refuse to fund a program at all.

After the legislature settles on a distribution and authorizes the state match, all funds are allocated to the DOW. For legal services, the DOW contracts with a state-level nonprofit corporation, similar to the national LSC, which administers the program.

Local programs are governed by a number of rules and regulations promulgated by the federal Department of Health and Human Services, the state DOW, and the State Legal Services Corporation (SLSC). Social Security Act, Title XX regulations primarily cover procedures to be followed in submitting a state plan and eligibility requirements for those serviced with these funds.[8] Contracts between the SLSC and local programs include requirements for client grievance procedures and eligibility that parallel LSC regulations, as well as prohibitions against handling fee generating and criminal cases.[9] Only state requirements for extensive activity reports from local programs differ from LSC rules and regulations.

Decisions regarding the distribution of funds to individual programs are made by a budget committee of the state corporation's board of directors. Unlike the LSC which funds according to a rigid formula, the budget committee of the state board has discretion regarding how much to allocate to each program. However, interviews conducted with members of the budget committee indicate that local programs in this state are funded at a level marginally higher or lower than the previous year, depending on the total amount allocated by the state legislature.[10] Thus, funding is not employed by the state board to influence activity at the local level. One member of the board summarized the criteria used in allocating funds:

> Budgetary determinations have never been tied to any substantive concern here. We've discussed the possibility of developing quality criteria, but it's

never gotten off the ground. . . . Our major decision rule is spread out the increases or decreases. Make sure all the programs gain or lose the same or similar amounts.

The nonprogrammatic use of funding allocations reflects the role perceptions of the SLSC and its board. State legal services officials do not conduct program evaluations. Inquiries about local operations only are made in response to specific complaints from clients, political officials, and others in the local community. SLSC staff see their role as maintaining salutary relations with the DOW and the legislature so that local programs continue to receive state funding. One veteran SLSC staffperson commented:

We don't try to tell programs what they should be doing. We never wanted a unitary program in this state. This program is structured to respond to diversity in local communities. Funding should only be used and in fact is only used to sustain programs, not to direct them.

Although the SLSC does not attempt to direct local program activities, the state legislature and the DOW share a clear preference for service work. For example, before writing the state plan the DOW requests information from local agencies regarding the number of clients they serve. The legislature also requests this information prior to allocating funds for legal services. Appearing before state legislative committees and in meetings with the DOW, SLSC officials are asked primarily about caseload numbers. This emphasis on servicing large numbers of clients is illustrated in the comments of one SLSC staffperson: "Without a doubt, legislators and the DOW want to know about numbers. 'How many people did you see this year?' This is what's important to them, you see."

THE PROGRAMS AND THEIR LOCAL ENVIRONMENT

Metro City Legal Services is the largest agency studied, employing some 70 lawyers scattered among a handful of offices. It services one county containing well over a million persons, approximately 12 percent of whom have incomes below the poverty line and 40 percent of whom are black. A large number of low-income advocacy groups surround the program and make demands on it.

Industrial Region Legal Services is nearly as large as MCLS, employing approximately as many lawyers, but scattered in more offices. The total population it services is nearly as large as that served by MCLS, but is dispersed among four counties. The population includes a smaller percentage of blacks (approximately 10 percent) and poor people (approximately 7 percent below the poverty line). Although IRLS is surrounded by many community organizations, few are advocacy oriented.

Suburban Legal Services employs ten lawyers and operates two offices. It services one county with a population of approximately 500,000, ranking its population in size between the metropolitan and rural areas. The population includes few poor people (3 percent below the poverty line) and blacks (approximately 4 percent). A few low-income organizations provide services and information to the poor, but no advocacy organizations are active. In contrast to the other four agencies, SLS receives a small amount of its funding, approximately $50,000, from the county government.

The two rural programs, Rustic Legal Services and Regional Rural Legal Services, are similar in many respects. Both employ a small number of lawyers—four in RLS and nine in RegRLS—and service communities containing relatively small populations. In both communities, approximately 9 percent of the population have incomes below the poverty line and less than 1 percent are black. Major differences in the two programs rest in the number of offices in operation and counties served. RLS operates one office that serves the poor in one county, while RegRLS has three offices—one in each of the counties it serves.

PROGRAM ACTIVITY

Several measures of program activity were used in this study. To measure the mobilization process lawyers were asked how they informed themselves about the problems of the poor in their communities. Table 3 shows that the responses vary significantly among programs. Because the number of responses fall below 25 in three agencies, the percentages reported should be interpreted with caution.

In MCLS, individual clients and community organizations are cited in equal proportions. Some MCLS lawyers gain knowledge of

Table 3
Mobilization Process by Program

Question: How are you informed about the legal problems of the poor in this community?

	Program									
Response	MCLS #Mentions	%	IRLS #Mentions	%	SLS #Mentions	%	RegRLS #Mentions	%	RLS #Mentions	%
Reactive:										
Clients	19	(35)	24	(67)	9	(75)	9	(90)	4	(100)
Proactive:										
Community groups	19	(35)	9	(25)	1	(08)	1	(10)	--	-----
Media	6	(11)	1	(03)	1	(08)	--	----	--	-----
Reports	3	(06)	--	----	--	----	--	----	--	-----
Government officials	3	(06)	--	----	--	----	--	----	--	-----
Client boards	2	(03)	--	----	--	----	--	----	--	-----
Other lawyers	1	(02)	2	(05)	--	----	--	----	--	-----
Social Service Agencies	1	(02)	--	----	1	(08)	--	----	--	-----
TOTAL	54 n=25		36 n=28		12 n=9		10 n=9		4 n=4	

poverty issues through independent readings of newspapers and reports written by public and private sources. Contacts with sympathetic government agency officials provide some MCLS lawyers with information regarding the enforcement of rights and laws or the implementation of social programs designed to benefit the poor. The mobilization process in the other four programs is less varied and more reactive than in MCLS. In IRLS, community organizations and other outside groups are cited much less often than in MCLS, with clients coming to the office constituting the major source of information. Clients are relied upon for information and problem definition to an even greater extent in SLS and RegRLS, and are the exclusive informational sources in RLS.

Figure 1 depicts the differences among agencies in their positions on a reactive-proactive continuum. Each agency's score derives from the difference in the percentage of reactive and proactive responses.[11] For MCLS, this figure is only 30, placing it close to the proactive pole. In sharp contrast, Rustic Legal Services shows a 100 unit difference and is considered a purely reactive program.

The mix of legal strategies employed by programs to resolve problems was measured in several ways. First, lawyers were asked to indicate the percentage of time they spent dealing with problems requiring reform strategies (i.e., law reform and lobbying) and service strategies (i.e., informal negotiation, *ad hoc* litigation). Table 4 reports the results.

Dramatic differences are shown among programs in the time spent on law reform and service. On average, MCLS lawyers spend the greatest amount of time engaging in law reform (41.8 percent), while RLS lawyers spend all of their time on service work. IRLS lawyers allocate more time to law reform (27.7 percent) than lawyers in the suburban and rural programs, but considerably less than MCLS. Of the nonmetropolitan programs, RegRLS spends the greatest amount of time (13.3 percent) on law reform.

The *Clearinghouse Review*, a monthly journal funded by the Legal Services Corporation, publishes detailed descriptions of "significant" law reform cases brought by legal services agencies, providing an alternative measure of strategies employed. Table 5 presents an analysis of cases printed in this journal between 1969 and 1982.[12]

Despite its crude nature, this measure confirms the interview data regarding activities. On average, more MCLS cases (20 per year) are

Figure 1
Program Position on Reactive—Proactive Continuum

```
             RLS   RegRLS   SLS     IRLS                  MCLS

Reactive     |-------X-------X-------X-------X---------------X---------------|   Proactive

             100     80      50      34      0               30             100
```

Percent Difference in Reactive and Proactive Responses

Table 4
Time Devoted to Law Reform by Program

	Number in Program				
Percent Time on Reform	MCLS	IRLS	SLS	RegRLS	RLS
0%	1	18	7	4	4
1-10	3	0	1	3	0
11-20	2	0	0	1	0
21-30	2	0	0	0	0
31-40	1	0	0	0	0
41-50	6	2	1	0	0
51-60	0	0	0	0	0
61-70	1	1	0	0	0
71-80	0	2	0	1	0
81-90	0	0	0	0	0
91-100	4	3	0	0	0
TOTAL	20	26	9	9	4
Mean[a]	41.8%	27.7%	6.1%	13.3%	0
Median[a]	50%	0%	0%	5%	0

[a] Figures based on raw data

printed than cases from any other agency in the study. Six cases per year from IRLS and less than one from RegRLS are printed. Only two from SLS and none from RLS appear in the journal in the entire 13-year period. MCLS lawyers brought nearly one-half of all cases

Table 5
Reform Cases Printed in *Clearinghouse Review*, 1969–1982, by Program

		Program					
Printed Cases	State-wide	MCLS	IRLS	SLS	RegRLS	RLS	Other
Number[a]	519	253	83	2	12	0	171
Average Number Per Year	40	20	6	0	9	0	12
Percentage of Total	100	49	16	0	2	0	33

[a]Cases appearing in more than one issue were counted as one case

printed from agencies located in this state, while IRLS and RegRLS lawyers brought 16 percent and 2 percent of the cases respectively.

The differences in work activities among the five programs are also confirmed by LSC evaluations and interviews conducted with government agency lawyers familiar with all of the programs in the state. The evaluations confirm the rank-order reported above, and without exception, government agency lawyers believe that MCLS engages in more law reform than any other agency in the state. IRLS lawyers are perceived to allocate some time to law reform, but not nearly as much as MCLS. Suburban and rural programs fall far below both of the metropolitan agencies. The comments of a deputy attorney general are typical of government agency lawyers' views:

I think I'm qualified to say this because I see all the litigation brought against the state and there is no other legal service organization over the years that has been able to bring anywhere near the volume of litigation against the state asking for broad kinds of changes that MCLS has. IRLS has brought a few, but even with those cases you find that it is not on the scale with the kinds of statewide stuff that MCLS does in Metro City.

The two chapters that follow provide an in-depth view of the operations of two programs varying significantly in size and activity. Chapter 4 describes the operations of Suburban Legal Services, a medium-sized program that primarily engages in service activity. This program is examined in detail to illustrate the variety of possible constraints on lawyers who wish to engage in social reform activity.

Chapter 5 examines Metro City Legal Services, one of the two largest programs studied. Attorneys in Metro City are the most proactive in mobilizing issues, and engage in more social reform activity than lawyers in the other four agencies. The in-depth look at this program illustrates the conditions under which poverty lawyers are relatively free of constraints in pursuing social reform. The case studies taken together describe the two basic models of legal services delivery found among the five programs studied. Subsequent to the two case studies, the remaining chapters assess the influence on activity across the five programs of personal, organizational, and interorganizational variables.

NOTES

1. In Appendix A of this work, I discuss the criteria used in selecting these sites and the methods employed in this study. Throughout the book, pseudonyms are used to refer to the programs because I felt it necessary to promise respondents that program names and locations would not be revealed. Shortly before I began the field work, the Reagan administration announced its intention to eliminate funding for the Legal Services Corporation. In such a political atmosphere, it seemed prudent to promise anonymity. I believe I would have been denied access to at least one program had I not given such assurances. Also, the quality and candor of lawyers' responses may have been affected had they believed that opponents of legal services could identify them or their program.

2. *Legal Services Corporation Act*, *U.S. Code*, title 42, sections 2809, 2971e, 2996–29961 (1974), Section 2996f (7).

3. Section 2996e (c) (2) (1974).

4. Section 2996f (a) (6a, 6b, 6c) (1974).

5. Section 2996f (b) (1974).

6. Section 2996i (c) (1974).

7. However, many supporters of the Legal Services Corporation feared that the board appointed by the Reagan administration would pass regulations restricting the activities of local programs. See Stuart Taylor, Jr., "Legal Aid Executive Quits, Citing Differences with Reagan's Board," *New*

York Times, December 3, 1982, A24, col. 3–4. Also see Mary Thornton and Pete Earley, "Inside the Legal Services Corporation," *Washington Post*, March 5, 1984, A21.

8. See 45 *C.F.R.*, section 228.

9. This discussion is based on contracts I obtained from the SLSC and interviews with SLSC officials.

10. Budgeting decisions of the state board conform closely to the incremental model discussed in Aaron Wildavsky, *The Politics of the Budgetary Process*, 3rd ed. (Boston: Little, Brown and Company, 1982).

11. Since community organizations are often clients of legal services programs, I did not assume *a priori* that their participation in issue definition differed from individual clients. Although in some circumstances community groups, like individual clients, bring specific problems to lawyers who then react, interviews with lawyers who represent groups indicated that the mobilization process typically is more intricate when organizations participate, acquiring many of the characteristics of a proactive process. This is discussed in more detail in Chapter 5.

12. All cases culled were brought by agencies in the state in which the five programs are located. Figures printed in Table 5 should be interpreted with caution because the journal prints cases in response to submissions by local program lawyers. The staff of the *Clearinghouse Review* makes no independent effort to identify law reform cases (telephone conversation with Lucy Moss, editorial staff of the *Clearinghouse Review*). While an admittedly crude measure of law reform effort, these data provide a check on the self-reported measure.

4

SUBURBAN LEGAL SERVICES: CONSTRAINTS ON POVERTY LAWYERS

Suburban Legal Services resides in a diverse county bordering Metro City. Its population of over 500,000 people is scattered among affluent bedroom communities, old manufacturing towns, and rural farm areas. Nearly 3 percent of its residents earn incomes below the poverty line and 4 percent are black. A smaller but growing hispanic population also resides in the county.

Inequalities of income and living conditions, quite visible to me during field visits, characterize Suburban County. Its per capita income of over $6,000 ranks it among the wealthiest in this state, but pockets of extreme poverty exist throughout the county.

Interviews conducted with a wide range of people holding various positions in the county indicated a local political system governed by a small number of interlocking elites. The major actors in county politics are leaders of the Republican Party, leaders of the local legal community, and the Republican county commissioners.[1]

Suburban County's politics are dominated by a Republican Party machine, reminiscent of the most effective urban machines in its nearly total control over local political life. The Republican Party's hegemony in Suburban County has not been challenged successfully since the late 1800s, so for the past century it has exerted tremendous control over the county's political agenda and its public sector jobs. In describing the Republican Party's power in Suburban County, the leader of the county's Democratic Party remarked: "The Republican Party just has had no serious opposition since I can remember. They see this county as their domain. I think you very much have the image of the victorian family exerting control over most aspects of life here."

Suburban County is very conservative politically. Nearly all candidates for public office run on platforms advocating low taxes and few expenditures and most extol the virtues of balanced budgets and limited government. In 1980 and 1984, Ronald Reagan captured over 60 percent of the popular vote, providing further evidence of the county's conservatism.

Unlike the bar associations of other counties examined in this study, the Suburban County Bar Association plays an important role in local politics. The bar's leadership generally emerges from the county's larger Republican law firms and many bar officials hold political offices and positions, such as party area chairman, city and county solicitors, county commissioners, and municipal councilman. This small set of leaders exerts a tremendous influence over the party's choice for judgeships and other county and municipal offices. Consistent with the county's general political climate, Suburban County's lawyer-politicians are conservative politically and typically select like-minded candidates for public office. A local judge commented on the role of the Suburban County Bar Association in local politics:

> We have a thousand members in our bar association, but the leadership is a relatively small group, 100 to 200 people, maybe less. Actually the real power structure, if you want to call it that, is considerably less than that. And many of these people are active on the outside in positions of political leadership. They are area leaders and public officials, that sort of thing. These people have had very significant roles in deciding who shall be a judge because of their political influence, not so much because of their position in the bar. But it happens that these people are very often directors of the bar association.

A lawyer echoed these themes:

> The bar association has respectability because of its political connections. I would say for the most part that the bar association is the child of the political party, the Republican Party. You have to go through the bar association to be considered judgeship material. You need the support of the leadership for many jobs in this county. You have to play their game. You

> have to go to their formal dinners and dances and make the necessary contributions. But you also have to be on the correct side of issues.

Suburban County's legal community enjoys close personal and professional relationships that are facilitated by family ties among lawyers, several formal committee meetings, and planned social activities held throughout the year. Consistent with the views of nearly all of the people interviewed, one Suburban Legal Services lawyer described the legal community as "a closed club . . . of private attorneys that are all tied with the Republican Party and the judiciary which is Republican." He continued, "It's like the good old boys and they all know each other and it's a lot of inbreeding and the same families that dominate the scene."

At the apex of Suburban County's power structure are the Republican members of the county commission. County commissioners are the chief county executives, making important decisions regarding the allocation of county funds and administering county programs. For as long as any of the interviewees in this county could remember, the Republican Commissioners were extremely conservative and the most powerful individuals in the county. Respondents described the current commissioners as skillful politicians who employ the budgetary process to exert control over all county agencies. One local political figure observed:

> The commissioners here are all-powerful. They have their fingers in every pie in the county. They give each agency less than they need and keep them guessing about their fate for the next year. This keeps everyone in line, you know. People in the county fear them.

Among the local folkways governing the behavior of Suburban County elites is an informal norm prohibiting divisive public debate. Rather than discussing grievances publicly, Suburban County elites prefer that settlement be sought in private. For example, a bench-bar conference is held periodically, providing members of both groups with an opportunity to discuss issues of common concern. Judges and members of the bar understand that areas of contention are to be held in confidence. The county commissioners and other public officials expect agency heads and private citizens to express criticisms of county policies to them in private, rather than through the media.

Consequently, nonelite groups and individuals rarely criticize local officials publicly or attempt to raise issues for public debate. In rare instances when challenges to established practices are voiced, Suburban County elites become deeply concerned. Because of the personal, professional, and political ties among elites, challenges to established policies and practices are viewed by those holding positions of power as challenges to all elites. In such cases, Suburban County's elites act in concert to manage and diffuse conflict. A community organizer working in Suburban County for a federal poverty agency discussed the reaction of elites to an attempt by her organization to raise a housing issue for public debate:

> The head of the housing authority is a very nice guy, a nice suburban gentleman. He'd be better off managing a private apartment complex or something. The head of employment services is good friends with him. They're all friends, all the agency and party people. And I tell you, you mess with one and the other one gets upset. They have ways of communicating that are amazing. We were bringing people to a county commissioner's meeting in regards to emergency housing. People needed housing and we wanted to speak at the meeting. Well, somehow the word gets out and the head of employment services calls up and says "I heard what you're planning. Did you tell the head of the housing authority about this?" I hadn't of course. You know, all of this is happening right before the meeting. Everybody finds out we're gonna be at the meeting.

Suburban County's poverty community is relatively unorganized and inactive politically. The poor are scattered throughout the county, increasing the difficulty in organizing countywide. A few low-income community groups exist, but they generally do not take public policy positions or lobby political officials. Direct action tactics, such as demonstrations, are rare because community organizers feel such methods are counterproductive in a county as conservative as Suburban. One of Suburban Legal Services paralegals described the poverty community as follows:

> Poor people here are not real organized. They lack leadership to a great extent. It's generally true in this county that you don't have a lot of yellers and screamers. The county gets upset if you yell and scream. Like if you go to the County Commissioners with something, they don't know what to do.

THE LAWYERS

Suburban Legal Services employs ten lawyers who work in two offices, one located a few blocks from the county courthouse and the other in an outlying area. Of the ten lawyers in the program, nine participated in this study. Only one attorney, a prison law specialist, had brought law reform cases to court.

Three of the nine lawyers came to the program directly from law school. Four others had worked in other legal aid or legal services programs, one moved from a large corporate firm in Metro City, and the other gained experience as an assistant city attorney in Metro City. On average, program attorneys were 32 years of age and possessed five years of legal experience. A majority (5 of 9) were born and raised outside of Suburban County.

A commitment to the poor and poverty or public interest law constituted the major reason that a vast majority (7 of 9) of Suburban Legal Services staff chose to work in a legal services program. At the other extreme, however, two of its lawyers accepted a job with legal services because it was their first, and in one case only, offer. The brief comments of two SLS lawyers regarding their motivations in seeking and accepting a job in a legal services program are typical of a majority of lawyers in this program.

> I specifically got into legal services work not because it was a job I could get, but because I wanted to direct my legal talents into an area that I philosophically found comfortable. This was such an area. . . . Criminal law was out because the criminal justice system seemed to come down harder on minorities and poor people than others. I didn't want to be involved in such a process. So this was a noncorporate, noncriminal endeavor and fit what I was looking for in the law.

> I went to law school intending to do something like legal services or some sort of public interest law. It's something I wanted for a long time. As long as I make an acceptable living, I prefer to do underdog work as opposed to standard general practice or corporation work. It's just an orientation I have.

The staff's commitment to poverty law is also illustrated in their career ambitions. A majority (5 of 9) hope to make a career of legal services work. Entering private practice is the ambition of four others, three of whom hope to remain in Suburban County.

A clear majority of Suburban Legal Services staff characterize their political beliefs as left-of-center and believe that their program should allocate more of its time and resources to social reform activity. Seven of nine lawyers identify their political values as left-of-center and five of nine prefer that the program devote at least one-half of its resources to law reform.[2]

Thus, even though a majority of Suburban Legal Services staff entered the program committed to poverty law, intend to remain in legal services, hold left-of-center political values, and advocate a more reform-oriented practice, the program engages almost exclusively in service to individual clients. Why isn't the activity mix of Suburban Legal Services more consistent with the motivations and personal predilections of its lawyers? The next section seeks to answer this question by examining constraints on the legal activity of program attorneys.

CONSTRAINTS ON LAW REFORM ACTIVITY

Program attorneys predisposed to engage in social reform activity are constrained by program policies and the local environment. Program policies, by and large, encourage service work and are important obstacles for lawyers wishing to engage in complex, time-consuming reform work. For example, only a few case categories that program attorneys are permitted to handle statutorily are excluded. Indeed, until 1980 the program accepted cases in all but three categories. In response to staff attrition, the number of case categories excluded increased to only fourteen by the time of my field visit.

Further, the program's director prohibited caseload adjustments for individual lawyers unless they are unable to handle all of their service cases. Lawyers are rarely excused from client intake. When they are removed from intake, it is for the purpose of clearing their files of excessive service cases, and not to permit them time to engage in law reform.

As a result of these policies, program staff struggle with heavy caseloads and have little time to devote to any particular case. Most reported handling between 75 and 125 active cases simultaneously. Comments of two staff lawyers illustrate the burdens imposed by large caseloads.

Most lawyers handle between 80 and 100 cases. There are people with larger numbers. People here have always had large caseloads. It doesn't mean we do a good job or that we're better than other programs. It's just that we don't have a union, so there's no one to say you can't handle more than 50.

Most people are on client intake once a week. And that's an afternoon a week, from one o'clock to four. I think most of us are in court three or four mornings a week which may spill over into the afternoon depending on how long the hearing goes. That's a busy schedule, to say the least.

The local environment also constrains the legal activity of Suburban Legal Services staff. Program attorneys without exception believe that cooperative relations with three local actors—the county commissioners, the bar association, and the judiciary—are essential. These groups are perceived as nearly monolithic, sharing attitudes regarding legal services and making similar demands on the program.

Why are these three groups perceived as important by program staff? Why do they believe it is essential to cultivate close relations with them? Cooperative relations are sought primarily because of their perceived importance to the program's survival, to individual lawyers within the program, and to indigent clients.

Staff believe that the program's continued survival depends on cooperative relations with and favorable evaluations by the county commissioners. The commissioners allocate nearly $50,000 to the program, a significant amount in the first few years of the program's existence because it was matched by the state government. Even though the state terminated matching funds in 1980, Suburban Legal Services personnel continue to value county funds, fearing that federal funds may be cut drastically or eliminated completely in the future. The comments of one program attorney illustrate the perceived importance of the commissioners for the program's survival:

The commissioners of course are important for practical political reasons. We get some funding from the county. I think we get about $46,000. That may not seem like much, but these days you never know about LSC funding. So if we get the county mad enough, I think there's a distinct chance we'd lose it.

Similarly, program staff perceive the local bar association and judiciary as important for the program's survival because of their potential influence on county funding decisions. Due to the legal community's ties to the county's majority political party, Suburban Legal Services staff fear that criticisms of their organization by the legal community could result in the county commissioners terminating their funding. Equally important, program personnel believe that a demonstration of close working relations with the court and the bar improves their image with county officials. One program lawyer remarked:

> One thing that's helped us a lot in funding, and it has been a tremendous help, is the number of our cases referred by the bench and bar. . . . There are hundreds of cases that come in here specifically referred by judges. In that situation, how can they then turn around and say that they don't need legal aid. Last year when ____ [the executive director] went to the county commissioners, he said X number of cases were referred specifically by a judge. And that surely helps.

Suburban Legal Services attorneys also seek cooperative relations with the legal community due to the assistance they may provide in case handling. Nearly all staff believe that cooperative relations facilitate negotiations, an important consideration for lawyers with heavy caseloads. Program staff stress the importance of "getting along" with the legal community in a county with a relatively small number of lawyers. Because Suburban Legal Services lawyers handle cases against particular opposing counsel quite frequently, poor working relations might result in unnecessary delays and court appearances. As one program attorney put it:

> It makes life a lot easier to be on good terms with the bar. It enables me to handle a lot more cases because I don't have to throw a lot of myself into smaller cases. They are more easily negotiated.

Four of the nine lawyers in Suburban Legal Services hope to enter private practice. To these lawyers, good working relations with the legal community are important for their career possibilities. Suburban Legal Services lawyers with an ambition to enter private practice believe that their prospects are enhanced if opposing counsel and judges view them as "reasonable" and "not overzealous." One Suburban Legal Service lawyer with an ambition to enter private practice remarked:

R. I do want to stay in Suburban County, preferably in this area. It's important to gain a reputation in this area as a good attorney because openings in this county seem to come about by word of mouth rather than by advertisements in a legal periodical.

Q. How do you go about gaining a reputation . . .

R. Well, you don't use the overzealous theory of representation in terms of dragging out a case that's obviously in an untenable position. Simply because you're a salaried individual and you don't have to worry about getting paid by your client, you decide to spend 3,000 hours on one case just to jerk somebody around or drag out a case that would not otherwise be dragged out. I think the private bar sees through that type of thing.

Finally, staff lawyers believe that cooperative relations with local lawyers and judges increase the likelihood of achieving satisfactory results for clients and fear that upsetting the legal community may result in adverse decisions. Indeed, one striking characteristic of lawyers in this program is their concern with the consequences of their actions for the future treatment of clients by the court and other agencies in the county. The following comments of one staff lawyer are typical.

I think one of the things we're concerned about here, especially any type of controversial action, is the ramifications of these actions on other individual clients we will bring into court. Going to the well or fighting to the last gasp over certain issues is not always the best strategy. We must sometimes balance this against . . . well, next week when we go into court with Mrs. Smith on a custody case is the judge gonna be so P.O.'d at us from the last week that things even unconsciously on his part are going to go against her. He's gonna say, "Oh, here comes that smart ass legal aid lawyer again. What's he gonna be unreasonable about now." And remember, we don't have that many judges here.

The groups that Suburban Legal Services depend on are opposed in no uncertain terms to law reform litigation. The county commissioners, for example, are concerned with lawsuits filed against county institutions, particularly those that may result in large public expenditures and negative publicity for county officials. These suits are viewed by the commissioners as indications of "disloyalty" because the program receives county funds. A Suburban Legal Services administrator and the Democratic county commissioner discussed the attitudes of the Republican commissioners:

> Clearly what they don't like is when this organization becomes an adversary. You can't have your cake and eat it too, I guess. . . . I don't think at least with _____ [the state prison], they care much at all. The county doesn't care much because it's a state institution. But county institutions are a different matter.
>
> Lawsuits against the county make them [the majority commissioners] furious. This is true especially for organizations that receive some county money. . . . They get upset about a number of things. First, of course, is the success of them. Some of these suits can cost the county a lot of money. But the other part is how much press does it get and how bad does it make everybody look. . . . The attitude of the commissioners is that they think these suits show no loyalty. You see, this county may be compared to a feudal village. It's a contract between the higher-ups and the lower-downs in a feudal system. The commissioners are very big on this. They get very upset when their subjects make things difficult for them.

Most officials and members of the Suburban County Bar Association prefer, for ideological reasons, that the program allocate its resources to individual client service and not to cases employing reform strategies. Members of the bar, by and large, are conservative and believe that social reform is not the province of a federally funded program. An official of the bar summarized its ideological makeup and attitudes regarding appropriate legal services lawyer behavior:

> Generally speaking, lawyers here are conservative. You have to remember that a tremendous number of our lawyers in Suburban County came from Metro City and one of the reasons is that they feel more comfortable here. Coming into a conservative county or a county with a conservative history . . . well, it encourages those who are more conservative to come in. Even those who are not so conservative tend to eventually meld in with the majority. And these people do not want a program here . . . that is Naderesque and tilts at windmills. No sir.

Suburban County's judges share the bar's ideological opposition to law reform litigation. Like the bar, Suburban County's bench is very conservative. Several judges who were interviewed referred to reform-oriented legal action disparagingly as "social engineering," "social campaigning," and "rabble rousing."

Judges also oppose social reform litigation for pragmatic political reasons. Like Suburban Legal Services, the local judiciary annually requests funding from the county. Due to their financial dependence on county officials, judges are sensitive to their concerns regarding any matter that relates to the court's operations, including lawsuits filed by Suburban Legal Services. In carrying out their judicial duties, then, judges consider the commissioners' concerns and at times speak with relevant parties on their behalf. Thus, lawyers who incur the wrath of the county commissioners can expect a similar response from the Suburban County bench. In a fascinating discourse on the politics of Suburban County's legal system, one judge described the relationship between the bench and county commissioners and the influence of the commissioners on the bench's behavior:

> Without going into detail, there are subtle ways that the executive branch—where it's a strong dominating branch—can effect every facet of county government. The simple fact is that the court has to go each year to the county commissioners with its budget requirements for the following year. . . . The reaction of the commissioners to a certain program or policy that might conceivably be within the power of the court to affect one way or another is taken into account. So that rapport, a good rapport between bench and county government, is necessary if things are going to run smoothly. And that sounds almost evil and obscene, as though there's some conspiracy between the court and the commissioners. It isn't that way. But I'm saying that the potential for that exists in these situations. . . . Sure we gauge some of our programs to what the commissioners, as the people who impose the millage on the taxpayers in this county, are able to swallow without getting themselves into difficulty. . . . When we decide how we're going to react to the way a legal aid program is working and one that the commissioners are having to fund, yes we're going to be susceptible to suggestions and that susceptibility will manifest itself in contact between us and the legal aid group which will then have an effect on them.

While Suburban County judges do not maintain regular social or professional contacts with the commissioners, they are able to anticipate their position on most issues that relate to the courts. The commissioners do not contact judges directly with regard to cases or issues before the court, but their public statements and comments by friends or associates are sufficient for the bench to comprehend quite clearly the commissioners' attitudes. The manner in which the commissioners' preferences are communicated to the bench is illustrated in the comments of a Suburban County judge:

> In the case of class actions being brought . . . let's say that in that case, the commissioners wouldn't discuss it directly or come to the court and say something like, "boy, what a vexatious situation," or something like that. We read the newspapers and would be aware of it. I guess it's a case where we would pretty much infer what the commissioners' attitude was going to be because without ever contacting us they would be making statements about it, in general, to the public or people who use the courts. Only an idiot would be unable to interpret. So we would get the message. And then we would look at the situation and indeed if it were out of hand or wasn't appropriate, the commissioners would achieve their end.

Law reform litigation and suits against county institutions are not the only types of legal activity opposed by Suburban County's judges. They also oppose legal actions against prominent members of the community. Consistent with the county's norm of resolving privately disputes involving prominent citizens and established institutions, the bench discourages lawsuits that may publicly embarrass members of the bar association, public officials, or taint the legal community.

How does the nature of Suburban Legal Services' political environment and their dependence on conservative local groups affect the legal representation provided by program lawyers to indigent clients? Interviews uncovered several avenues available to relevant Suburban County groups in their attempts to influence attorneys' strategic decisions. In general, these avenues are employed successfully to constrain the use of reform strategies and the handling of potentially controversial cases.

The county commissioners, bar association, and judges exert influence on Suburban Legal Services lawyers in a variety of ways. First, they communicate to the program and members of its governing board of directors their feelings about particular legal actions and possible negative consequences for the program if these actions proceed. For example, Suburban Legal Services brought a lawsuit against the county jail, an institution described by one Suburban County judge as "medieval." The lawyer bringing the suit asked a federal court to order general improvements in the jail, improvements sure to prove costly to the county. The commissioners immediately convened a meeting to discuss methods of pressuring

Suburban Legal Services to drop the lawsuit. The Democratic commissioner explained:

> The majority of commissioners were fit to be tied that among the suits brought against them, one was brought by an attorney from legal aid.... And their first reaction was, "And how much money have we given them? This has got to stop. What can we do to cut their feet off?" We really had a serious discussion in there with the solicitor as to what we could do about it. And the solicitor... felt that the members of SLS's board were reasonable people.... I think they know that you get further in a community like this if you don't come across like ____ [a community activist from Metro City known for the use of militant tactics]. And so, the solicitor felt we should try to get to the board.

Subsequent to this meeting, the commissioners dispatched the county solicitor to meet with members of the program's governing board and the commissioners personally contacted the lawyer responsible for the suit. In both cases, the commissioners threatened funding cuts if the lawsuit proceeded through the courts. A member of the governing board and the lawyer bringing the suit described the pressures exerted by the commissioners:

> We've been under a lot of pressure. Threats, outright bold threats from the county commissioners.... They are in no way subtle. I've had meetings where an attorney on our board says, "such and such called. He wants to have a meeting." This person who called was the right-hand man of the commissioners, the county solicitor. We had a meeting for an hour. He said, "We don't like you suing the county because of the prison situation." ____ [the executive director] is squeamish about it. He wants to keep a good rapport with the county.

> The prison suit that I brought is asking for upgrading conditions. The county commissioners called me and said they felt that their money was better spent on legal aid than on building a new prison. That was pretty straight-forward.

In some instances, Suburban County's judges communicate their demands directly to program personnel. In one case, for example, the bench was upset with a Suburban Legal Services' lawsuit filed in federal court against a former bar association official. Concerned that this suit might generate negative publicity for the legal community, Suburban County's President Judge met with the program's director, expressed his concerns, and the case was dropped. One administrator recalled:

Apparently the biggest concern was that the President Judge indicated that it was bad publicity for the bar association, and though there might be merit to the suit, he would appreciate it and was advising our director for future reference to be contacted to see if something couldn't be informally worked out. In other words, don't make bad publicity for us. Talk to me first. If Joe Blow did something wrong, we'll sit down with him and work something out. But it doesn't have to make the ______, the ______, and _____ [three newspapers], all in the same day. Yea, we get called on the carpet here. Maybe more so than in a lot of counties.

In other cases, judges and members of the bar communicate their demands to a bar association official who sits on the program's governing board. When problems arise, this lawyer acts as a liaison between the legal community and the program. In most cases, suggestions and demands are considered carefully by the program. The legal community's liaison on the program's board explained:

I have been the buffer between certain unhappiness in the bar, whether it was the bar or bench, and legal aid. And I will say this, the executive director has cooperated tremendously because he's a pragmatist too. . . . But _____ [the executive director] understands that the facts of life are that you have to listen and he does. . . . What they have suggested is in the class action area, that sort of thing. Only when it gets on the cause level have I had to step in and meet with _____ [the executive director]. It's not that often by the way. I would say that possibly twice a year I have to be that buffer and work between the two groups.

To influence the behavior of program attorneys, the commissioners and legal community need not communicate their demands and threaten the program on a regular basis. The attitudes of conservative groups and the possibility of retribution for reform oriented legal action are understood quite clearly by Suburban Legal Services lawyers. In choosing cases and legal strategies, program staff anticipate the reactions of salient conservative groups and seek to avoid confrontation. The county jail suit was the only one of its kind brought by the program. The general posture is to avoid engaging in potentially controversial, headline-producing activity. Program administrators and several staff lawyers openly discourage the bringing of lawsuits with a potential to incur the wrath of county elites. For example, one lawyer reported that the program's executive director prohibited the filing of a lawsuit against the county's Children and Youth office for violations of procedural safeguards in custody hearings. Another lawyer reported that colleagues in the office discouraged his filing suit against a county judge in his role as landlord. In all, five of the nine lawyers in the program discussed with me at least one instance when a lawsuit with reform potential was not filed due to fears of adverse political consequences.

While Suburban Legal Services staff and administrators are wary in general of engaging in law reform activity, program administrators are concerned particularly that no potentially controversial actions are initiated during the fall and winter months when the commissioners consider their budget request. Attorneys are instructed to avoid bringing these actions until late winter, after the program has received its yearly appropriation. One administrator explained this policy:

> I think we usually go before the commissioners sometime in September and October. And I think that ____ [the executive director] always indicated to ____ [the prison law specialist] to try not to turn up the jets any time in the fall, right before we go for money. If you feel that it's necessary to go before judge so and so in federal court to cite the county for contempt and dragging their heels with the prison, please don't do it until February.

Due to its service orientation and cooperative posture, the program gained the support of judges and members of the bar association. The legal community by and large expressed satisfaction with Suburban Legal Services' operations and praised their efforts on behalf of indigents. Judges and private lawyers who were interviewed considered program staff as full-fleged members of the legal community. Further, the legal community seemed to feel a closeness to the program unique among the programs examined in this study. Unlike other programs, where the legal community perceived legal services lawyers as outsiders or in various ways different from private practitioners, Suburban County judges and private lawyers often referred to them as "*our* legal aid lawyers." Interestingly, several members of the legal community expressed opposition to continued funding for the national Legal Services Corporation, but supported its local grantee. The comments of a local judge, though perhaps more colorful, are typical of judges' and lawyers' views:

R. I'd love to see the Legal Services Corporation die. I think that corporation is totally off base. The corporation went far beyond the concept of providing legal services to people who needed it, who were indigent. I think they began to look at law as some sort of avocation and their real avocation was to change American society in ways they felt it should be changed. . . . And of course the other thing is that a lot of the people who gravitate towards that organization are the kooks in the profession. . . . As soon as you have a government-funded program with lots of money . . . all the leftwing kooks seem to gravitate towards that. I'm sure there are not six registered Republicans in the whole damn . . . operation. And that being the case, as a good rightwing Republican, I say I'm not going to support these people who are trying in my mind to tear down the appropriate pillars of society.

Q. How do you feel about Suburban Legal Services?

R. I think it works. The people who are involved in it are dedicated. They do their job. They know they're here to provide one on one legal services for people who can't afford legal services otherwise.

LOCAL DISSATISFACTION WITH PROGRAM OPERATIONS

Although Suburban County's poverty community is relatively unorganized and generally passive, a few community organizers working for federal poverty agencies located in the county attempt to organize the poor and raise issues of concern to them. Unlike judges and private lawyers, community organizers expressed some dissatisfaction with the activities of Suburban Legal Services attorneys. For one thing, community organizers criticized the program's lack of enthusiasm for community work and organizing. One organizer commented:

They don't get involved with community problems. The only way they'll get involved is if I beg them to come to meetings. _____ [the executive director] will usually send someone if I ask but, you see, they should have a closeness with the community. I shouldn't have to coax them to come.

Community organizers also criticized the program's reluctance to confront the county government. In one much discussed, highly visible case, a handful of the poor led by a community organizer attended a meeting of the county commissioners to complain about a lack of emergency housing. The organizer was furious with Suburban Legal Services' unwillingness to send an attorney to accompany the group. In discussing this case, the organizer remarked:

> The problem here is that people are afraid to deal with them that has power. _____ [the executive director] and me are good friends, but he likes to keep a low profile. He would rather I raise the hell and his lawyers stay in the background. For example, there was a landlord in _____ who was not providing heat to his tenants. . . . There was a program approved by the county commissioners a couple of years earlier for emergency housing. There was supposed to be money for just such a case. This money was never available. I had people coming into my office without heat. They were living in cold houses. Well, we went down to the commissioners meeting. We looked around and there were no legal aid lawyers. They knew what we were going to do. We thought they'd be there. So you see a lot of agencies, including legal aid, are afraid of the county. Legal aid is worried about their funding. Now, I understand that. He has problems with the bar and the county. But I don't agree with the policy of not getting involved with the community.

SUMMARY

The Suburban Legal Services case illustrates quite well the variety of potential constraints on poverty lawyer activity. Despite the predisposition among a majority of Suburban Legal Services staff to initiate law reform litigation, program policies promoting heavy caseloads and their reliance on local organizations opposed to law reform influence their decisions on legal strategy and affect their activity mix.

The local environment seems to be a particularly powerful influence on program attorneys. The program operates in a tightly controlled county governed by conservative political and legal elites. These political actors do not hesitate in making substantive demands on the program regarding cases to handle or avoid and legal strategy. By and large, program staff fear the political consequences of generating controversy through the filing of class action suits, test cases in appellate courts, and lawsuits against county institutions. The remarks of two program lawyers, one who has brought a few law reform suits and one who has not, illustrate the crucial influence of Suburban County's conservative political climate and power structure on legal representation.

> In this program there are not enough people taking aggressive stands. I think people are intimidated by the tremendous political clout that is wielded by the Republican Party in this county and they cowtow to that. They are in mortal fear of that power.
>
> In taking a class action suit or a suit against the county, I'm afraid quite frankly of what the repercussions may be down the line. It may have some damage on my career, for example. I could think of all kinds of things.

The salience of Suburban Legal Services' environment is shown further by the remarks of one member of the program's governing board. When asked to speculate on the consequences for the program of engaging in activities similar to the more reform-oriented program in neighboring Metro City, he responded:

> Oh! They would have been bombed out. Well, the water would have been cut off. They wouldn't get electricity. They would have immediately had no more county funding. The bar association would probably claim that all the lawyers never passed the bar and were not certified to practice before any court of law. They would go berserk if they had Metro City Legal Services up here. . . . If legal aid in Suburban County were anything like that, half, 25% like that, ah, their lease would have been cancelled. They would have found some clause to cancel the lease. And then when they sued over the lease, the judge over in the courthouse would say, "Nope. Looks like a valid reason to me. Out."

NOTES

1. In Suburban County, three commissioners are elected. Only two may be of the same political party. So, for many years, the Suburban County commission has been composed of two Republicans and one Democrat.
2. The precise ways in which characteristics of lawyers and programs were measured are discussed in Chapters 6–8.

5

METRO CITY LEGAL SERVICES: FREEDOM TO PURSUE LAW REFORM

Metro City is a large commercial center ranking among the twenty most populous metropolitan areas. Over 10 percent of its population earn incomes below the poverty line and a large black population is active politically. Massive ghetto areas overlay nearly one-half of Metro City's land area and are characterized by racial segregation. Race has been a salient issue in Metro City politics for many years.

A dense and richly varied array of groups have evolved that are active participants in the city's political life. Citywide and neighborhood-based low-income organizations of all types are active. Differing greatly in goals and methods, these groups range from social service organizations to community development corporations and advocacy groups. Although students of urban politics note the decline of low-income advocacy organizations in the 1970s, a large number of such groups remain active in Metro City.[1] Indeed, these organizations are a significant force in local politics. Several community groups are allied closely with state and local political officials and an increasing number of community activists have gained elective office.

Low-income advocacy groups are concerned with several general issue areas, most commonly welfare, housing, consumerism, and education. They typically organize citywide, though a few are neighborhood-based. A few active groups, such as the Association of Community Organizations for Reform Now (ACORN), are local branches of national organizations. Most, however, originate locally. Tremendous competition exists among low-income groups for members, resources, and publicity.

In several of the citywide groups, blacks play important leadership roles. These groups tend to have a predominantly black membership, although many receive crucial financial and political support from predominantly white, politically liberal organizations.

On the other hand, Metro City's neighborhood groups tend to be composed of white, working-class ethnics. Many of these groups organized to exclude blacks and hispanics from their neighborhoods and their political activity centers on opposing policies, such as public housing, advocated by citywide groups. Neighborhood groups engage in other types of activity, such as crime patrols, beautification campaigns, and social affairs.

Confrontation and conflict characterize Metro City politics, due in large part to the spatial segregation of its residents and their organization along racial lines. Community organizations frequently employ direct-action strategies, such as boycotts, picketing, and other forms of demonstration, to achieve their goals. This is especially true for citywide organizations, as evidenced in the comments of one Metro City Legal Services attorney:

> Community groups let people know how they feel about issues. Citywide groups in particular tend to be confrontative. They use confrontation as a good technique and they've developed that to an expertise. A lot of them are not afraid to get arrested.

Unions play an important role in Metro City politics, with public employee and service industry unions showing exceptional strength. Although many unions are parochial in their concerns, lobbying primarily for increased wages and better working conditions, some had become involved in issues affecting the poverty community. For example, during my field visit, a powerful union of hospital workers threatened to strike several local hospitals to protest Reagan Administration budget cuts in health care programs for the poor.

Metro City's media, particularly its newspapers, provide extensive coverage of low-income issues and their editorial positions are often sympathetic to the problems of the poor and the tactics of low-income advocacy groups. For example, the major morning and evening newspapers had for many years focused attention on a low-income housing shortage and supported editorially a squatting campaign of housing groups concerned with this issue.

THE LAWYERS

At the time of my field research, Metro City Legal Services employed over 70 lawyers scattered in a number of neighborhood offices and one central city location. Lawyers in the central city office are excused from regular client intake so that they may devote a substantial portion of their time to developing reform issues and strategies. In contrast, attorneys in neighborhood offices handle a larger volume of cases, interviewing clients regularly. All offices in the program assign lawyers to specialized units (e.g., consumer, welfare, housing). Lawyers in nearly all offices engage in some social reform activity. Of the over 70 lawyers in the program, a sample of 25 was chosen for analysis.[2]

Most of the lawyers in my sample (19 of 25) entered legal services directly upon graduating from law school, but several (6 of 25) spent some time after graduating working for community groups, such as local welfare rights and consumer groups. The Vista program placed a few of these attorneys with community groups and others volunteered their time and service. Each of the six lawyers reported maintaining contacts with these groups subsequent to gaining employment with legal services.

On average, Metro City Legal Services attorneys are 33 years of age and possess seven years of legal experience. A small core of lawyers had worked in the program since its establishment in the mid–1960s. The impressive amount of legal experience that program lawyers possess contributes to their ability to spot reform issues and fashion broad reform strategies. One veteran government agency lawyer put it like this:

> Let me tell you something about MCLS that might be useful to you. They hired many of their lawyers in the sixties and have the advantage of having kept those people. I've been here for eight and a half years and they've been there ten years or certainly damn near ten. Yea, they've got a real good sense by now of where the bodies are buried.

By and large, program lawyers are very committed to poverty law, as evidenced not only by the fact that so many have remained with the program over the years but also by the reasons for which they chose a legal services job. The older, more experienced lawyers entered legal services in the 1960s and early 1970s. Influenced by the political atmosphere of the period, they typically went to law school with a clear intention of working in legal services or other public interest organizations and only applied for jobs of this nature. The comments that follow are typical of the program's more experienced attorneys.

I graduated from ______ law school in '69. I applied for no jobs other than legal services. That was a period when there was a lot of political action. The poverty program was getting off the ground. The Peace Corps was young and glorious. And you know, poverty was a war. And it was a much more important war than Vietnam. There was no choice. I had no particular interest in helping the rich get richer. I saw some significant issues, real intellectual challenges in legal services. So I went to work for legal services in ______ in 1969.

I graduated from ______ in 1968. I went to school at a time when people were looking for things to do in terms of making life better for the poor. The reason I decided to go to law school was so I could work for a legal services program. That's what I had in mind. That was my goal.

Younger, more recently hired program staff differ from veterans in some important respects. Most of them were unaffected by the social movements and political climate of the sixties and entered legal services for a variety of reasons, including a preference for a relaxed work environment, the opportunity to gain immediate courtroom experience, and a general feeling of obligation to the poor. Most mention a commitment to the poor as one reason for seeking a legal services position, but they do not link their commitment to broader political goals or movements, as do many of the veterans. One veteran summarized differences among program staff in the following terms:

By and large, the older turkeys who are still here came to this for the same reason they went to law school in the first place. A lot of us didn't go to law school because we were out to make our first million by the time we were 28. We went to law school to be doing something socially useful, something that would promote what we thought were goods in the world. . . . A lot of the younger people, I don't know why they're here. Many times

I've asked them, "what the hell are you doing here anyway? You should be out in private practice making money."

The stability and continuity that an older, experienced staff provides promises to continue into the future. When asked about career goals and ambitions, program lawyers overwhelmingly state that they intend to remain with the Metro City program. Only seven of the lawyers in the sample hope to leave the program for other types of legal work, and of the seven, only two hope to enter private practice in Metro City.

Politically, program attorneys clearly are left-of-center. Indeed, 87 percent of lawyers in the sample characterize their beliefs as "liberal" or "left-of-liberal," with a majority viewing themselves as "left-of-liberal." Over one-half of the sample prefer a social reform orientation for legal services programs. Thirty-two percent advocate an equal mix of service and law reform, while only 14 percent prefer an emphasis on service to individual clients.

Unlike Suburban Legal Services, the activity mix of the Metro City program is more or less consistent with the motivations and personal predilections of its staff. The next section explores some of the reasons why.

FREEDOM TO PURSUE LAW REFORM

In sharp contrast to Suburban Legal Services, program policies and aspects of the local environment combine to provide Metro City attorneys with the freedom to pursue social reform. Program policies, for example, provide program staff with the time needed to prepare complex litigation. Program lawyers are unionized, giving them some control over many policies affecting work activities. One particularly significant union contract provision permits lawyers to petition for caseload adjustments when overburdened with cases. The provision requires management personnel to consider several criteria when deciding on these claims—"the number of open and active cases, complex litigation, active group representation, and legislative and administrative advocacy work."[3] The petitioning process, invoked successfully by several lawyers interviewed, protects lawyers with a desire to engage in law reform from the obstacles imposed by cumbersome caseloads found in many legal services programs.[4]

Three sets of actors shape policies within the program regarding which case types are handled and excluded. First, the governing board excludes several case categories for all offices, such as wage claims, name changes, property settlements, negligence and tort claims, several types of child visitation cases, and traffic offenses. Each neighborhood office constructs its own list of excluded categories and, finally, each substantive specialty unit in several offices has additional exclusions. Along with the adjustment policy, the three tiered exclusion process protects lawyers against overwhelming caseloads and makes it difficult for management personnel to know what cases are handled at a particular time throughout the program.

After lawyers accept cases, they enjoy nearly total discretion in choosing strategies. Lawyers report little supervision in case handling, as evidenced in the comments of one attorney:

> One of the good things about this program is that there has been the flexibility to go after the kinds of things you want. That's been an advantage of the sort of loose organization that has typified this program. There aren't any barriers to people getting involved in major litigation or in learning other areas of the law.

In addition to giving the lawyer time to engage in law reform, program practices encourage it. For many years, the governing board and executive director requested from staff lists of "significant" cases handled and law reform victories.[5] Although lawyers are not rewarded in salary or promotions for law reform work, a measure of performance with a preference for law reform developed within the organization. One attorney explained:

> No one says, "do law reform." But the board and _____ [a previous director] wanted to see every month what you'd done in the area of impact. So people around here came to believe that this was the way to go.

The value placed on law reform contributed to personal animosities between neighborhood and central office lawyers. Many neighborhood office lawyers believe that "hotdogs" in the central office do less work and receive more credit and respect than they. Many refuse to inform central office lawyers about potential or planned litigation, fearing that they will "snatch" or "steal" interesting cases.[6] One program administrator provided an overview of the tensions among lawyers:

> Because they [central office lawyers] don't have a specific geographical area to serve, they don't have the client demand that you get in the neighborhoods. So in terms of the sexy part of lawyering, you find that more down here in the central office than you will in the neighborhoods. It's created a lot of animosity in the program. . . . Also, there is the unfortunate perception out in the neighborhoods that some of the lawyers down here will take over a case if they tell the lawyers about it or ask any questions about how to handle it. So many of these folks won't call down here for help because they believe someone will snatch their case.

Some of the animosity between neighborhood and central office attorneys stems from the allocation of credit for cases submitted and published in law reform journals, such as the *Clearinghouse Review*. Cases are often submitted by central office lawyers in their role as directors of specialty units. Some lawyers in neighborhood offices report not receiving appropriate credit as lead counsel on cases in which they do much of the work, charging that central office lawyers claim credit to enhance their reputations as law reformers. As one neighborhood lawyer put it:

> All you have to do is read the *Clearinghouse Review* and you see the ego thing that takes place here. We had an attorney here who was working on a case in which he did most of the work. He put in the hours. He appeared in court. But when the notice appeared in the *Clearinghouse Review* his name was like third on the list. . . . A downtown lawyer more or less came in on the case and took all the credit. . . . The whole idea is, you send a case down and you forget it. But if you've got a client that will help them in one of their cases, they'll let you come in on the case and give you a few crumbs from the table. But they're gonna go for all the glory.

In contrast to Suburban Legal Services, Metro City Legal Services' environment permits and, in certain respects, encourages law reform activity. A variety of external organizations with conflicting preferences surround the program. Conservative organizations, such as the state court bench and segments of the bar association, prefer that legal services programs allocate its resources to individual client service and avoid heavy investments in social reform activity. On the other hand, low-income advocacy organizations prefer law reform to service. In such an environment, Metro City Legal Services staff may choose which set of groups to rely upon for critical resources.

With few exceptions, program staff chose low-income groups as allies, citing them as the most important external source of support and cooperation. Some lawyers mention particular organizations they had worked with over the years, while others cite community groups more generally. The following comments are typical of lawyers' views.

> I think all of our group clients are persons we want to have a favorable relationship with. They are the life blood of the program.

> Good relations with community groups are essential. This program has been built over the years—and it's one of the oldest in the country—with this kind of relationship with a broad spectrum of community groups around the city.

Program lawyers chose community groups as allies for several reasons. First, low-income groups are viewed as natural allies for ideological reasons. A majority of program staff hold left-of-center political values and are sympathetic to the political goals of these groups.

However, cultivating their support and cooperation is important to program staff for other reasons. In general, lawyers value the various types of support and resources offered by low-income groups. For example, some lawyers value the social support they provide, and perceive community groups as more likely than individual clients to demonstrate appreciation for the lawyer's efforts. One veteran lawyer explained:

> To a lawyer it means a lot because if I get any praise at all, it generally comes from a group as opposed to an individual client. And it means more if a group like the Welfare Rights Organization says, "this is my lawyer and he does a good job," than for an individual welfare recipient who has gotten her checks replaced. The individual client may mean something to some attorneys, but you ordinarily don't get feedback from the individual. We get it from groups, both good and bad, so I think it's important.

Program staff appreciate the critical role community groups play in mobilizing issues. Several attorneys confer regularly with poverty community leaders, discussing among other things problems common to the residents. As one lawyer put it:

> The relationship with community groups actually predates my coming to MCLS, but it's been cultivated by the need to be kept abreast of what's going on out in neighborhoods in terms of the issues that directly affect them or greatly affect their membership.

Although in some cases community groups alert program lawyers to problems in their neighborhoods, typically the mobilization process involves the participation of both lawyers and community groups. In these situations, attorneys value the more limited role community groups play. The dynamics of Metro City Legal Services' mobilization process are illustrated by the comments of two veteran lawyers:

> In rate increase cases, I generally represent the same clients year after year. And those are three community groups with whom I work regularly, ACORN, Metro City Consumers, and Senior Citizens for Justice. We are in constant touch discussing a whole range of problems, most of which never come to formal cases. I probably talk with them an average of three times a week, at least.... They might call up and say, "did you hear that such and such is going to happen? What do you recommend?" Occasionally, I will call them and say, "do you know that such and such is about to happen and this is going to affect you?"

> Three or four people may come in with the same medical assistance problem and I may win each one of those at a hearing or resolve it by negotiations. All of a sudden I say, "gee, why do three or four people have the same problem?" A group will say, "you dummy, it's happening all over." It legitimizes looking broader than these three or four people.

Program lawyers secure government agency handbooks and other literature from community groups, which provide them with a better understanding of agency procedures and people to contact when faced with administrative error, delay, or enforcement problems. As one welfare specialist explained:

> This may sound extremely inconsequential, but I would dare say that most legal services offices do not have telephone directories for the welfare de-

partment. Bureaucracies frequently don't like to give out this information and having it saves a tremendous amount of time. . . . A community group can just demand a copy and say, "oh, and send a copy to my lawyer." That's one of the benefits that we've long enjoyed.

Several program lawyers rely on the files of community groups for information regarding such things as welfare department enforcement policies, housing conditions, and Housing Authority admission practices. This information alerts lawyers to potential problems and may be used in writing complaints, outlining the factual basis for lawsuits, and providing a rationale for legislative and administrative advocacy. One attorney remarked:

These groups do a lot of work around issues that concern them, like the condition of housing, vacancy rates, and utilities. They have records that although not conclusive in themselves can lead to other things. This information can lead you down a path that you haven't considered.

Further, by identifying individuals victimized by laws or practices, community groups assist attorneys in overcoming typical obstacles in class action litigation. Prior to court certification of a class, government agencies and private institutions named as defendants often attempt to mollify plaintiffs by correcting the problem for the few individuals named in order to avoid the possibility of being held liable for broad-based relief that could result from successful litigation. Metro City Legal Services attorneys are able to circumvent these attempts by defendants, as one lawyer explained:

They have access to people who could be plaintiffs. You know, like sometimes you file a class action and your plaintiffs get bought off. What do you do next? The court might say we must dismiss the case because its moot. You know it shouldn't be dismissed because there are thousands of people out there with the same problem but every time one, two, or three of them come to you they get moved to better housing or have their place repaired. These groups can be an important source of plaintiffs to intervene in these suits.

Community organizations also assist program lawyers in problem resolution by pressuring relevant officials to settle suits involving broad policy questions. A lawyer who filed a major lawsuit seeking to place the Metro City Housing Authority in receivership commented:

> Take this big case with the Housing Authority. You know from the start that this kind of class action lawsuit is going to be highly contested. It's gonna take a much broader approach, broader than a lawyer simply filing a suit. We need help. It's gonna take group confrontation. It's gonna take a tremendous amount of pressure from groups on political individuals because its a political animal to begin with—the Housing Authority.

Community groups also play an important role in Metro City Legal Services internal politics. The more militant organizations, in particular, have gained much influence over internal policy. For example, due to annual uncertainties regarding funding for legal services, program staff are concerned with personal job security and the fate of their particular office. Over the years, rumors have circulated throughout the program about impending budget cuts, layoffs, and office shutdowns. In the early 1980s, these rumors became more meaningful when the program's board of directors held meetings to determine how to "restructure" in the face of almost certain budget cuts. Lawyers with ties to community groups mobilized clients to protect their organizational turf. For example, the program's director sought to institute a centralization program whereby all neighborhood offices would consolidate in a central city location. Neighborhood office lawyers mobilized group clients and demonstrations commenced outside the central administration office until the board and the program's director abandoned the plan. Similarly, one neighborhood office created to serve Metro City's hispanic population remained open after several attempts by the administration to eliminate it. Many lawyers attributed the office's resilience to the power of hispanic groups in this neighborhood. As one lawyer put it:

> These groups were very vocal in getting that office established. They've been vocal in keeping it open against all good sense and odds. We really don't have bilingual people to staff it. It's a political situation. The usual sorts of forces and laws apply, you know. Confrontation politics has been employed against MCLS just as MCLS clients have often employed it against others.

It is significant that the administration at this time chose to eliminate the only office in the program without support from militant community groups. In an interview, the managing attorney of this office discussed his "philosophical opposition" to the tactics employed by these groups and suggested that his office's role was to represent individual clients. In response to this posture several militant organizations lobbied actively for the elimination of this office. The managing attorney summarized his dilemma in an interview conducted with him two months prior to the board's decision.

> I've been in contact with many groups and civic associations. But these squatter groups say I only deal with middle class groups. They say I've not been dealing with grassroots people. . . . That's hurt us. For example, there's the Housing Action Group. Their viewpoint of us is completely, totally negative. And that's important because they went to a board meeting and testified strongly that this office should be closed immediately. . . . I refuse to let them affect our day to day operations here and now they want this office closed forthwith, without any hesitation.

Thus, it is important for program lawyers to gain the respect and cooperation of community groups because of their influence on internal policy. Indeed, due to close relations between lawyers and politically powerful community groups, coalitions of lawyers and group leaders shape internal policy decisions. A program administrator readily acknowledged the influence of these coalitions.

> A good example . . . is with the priority-setting process. The energy project is a three-attorney unit that handles a series of cases, including utility rate cases. Now one of their major clients is ACORN. I had recommended to the Client Service Committee of our board that they no longer be given this responsibility. . . . ACORN felt that was one of their priorities. They came in and were huffy about my recommendation. This was probably instigated by the attorney. . . . In assignment of cases, if an attorney dislikes an assignment that has been given him and they feel that it's in conflict with an obligation to a group, they'll generally get the group to call me up and put pressure on me. . . . Each unit within MCLS has a corresponding ally on the outside in the form of a community group that it not only provides legal services for but uses to pressure the administration. . . . Groups are important and powerful in the sense that they do sway judgments here within MCLS on certain issues and involving certain attorneys.

Finally, program staff value the funding support community groups provide. Because several community groups maintain close ties to certain politicians in the area, they are perceived as influential in the funding process. One program attorney explained:

> One thing we try to do is satisfy our group clients enough with the quality of legal services so that they will communicate that to their legislators. And we have fortunately been in the position of representing some of the larger community groups. . . . You see, our group clients are politically active, politically aware, and very astute politically. They know what to do, who to do it to, and they do it.

Objectively, community group support for Metro City Legal Services' activity seems important in explaining the program's survival. Over the years, several lawsuits filed by program attorneys had been quite visible and occasionally controversial. A successful suit to force a recalcitrant city government administration to construct a previously planned public housing project in a predominantly white, working-class neighborhood is perhaps the most widely publicized and criticized action. Program lawyers also brought a series of successful suits leading to the creation and implementation of an affirmative hiring and promotion plan for blacks in the state police force. In housing, Metro City Legal Services lawyers filed several actions against the Metro City Housing Authority, culminating in a broad-based class-action lawsuit requesting that the authority be placed in receivership. In short, most of the powerful individuals and institutions in Metro City—including mayors, city councilmen, universities, judges, and prison wardens—have been at some time the target of a lawsuit filed by the program.

These types of lawsuits have engendered political opposition from several external groups and organizations. For example, in the late 1970s, several members of the city council charged the program with representing "political organizations," in violation of the Legal Services Corporation Act. Further, each year state legislators publicly complain about the program's legislative advocacy activities. In 1981, the state's governor blamed Metro City Legal Services for a prison riot and hostage-taking because the leader of the inmates had been released from solitary confinement several years earlier due to a lawsuit filed by a program lawyer. In each of these cases, community groups along with state legislators allied with them publicly supported the program's activity. The comments of a state welfare department lawyer vigorously opposed to the program's law reform work suggest that this support is critical for the program's continued survival.

> I'm pro-legal services, but anti-MCLS. I voice my opposition and my complaints and my bitching to the Secretary of Welfare regularly. I've suggested on several occasions that the state stop funding them. Why doesn't the state do it? Well, I can just see it now. All those people rushing up here on buses to sit-in and demonstrate. All the theatrics and shit that goes with it and these people saying, "you're cutting the only legal services program with teeth." It is not really possible politically.

Relationships between program lawyers and low-income groups not only provide the program with needed political support and assistance in designing and implementing reform strategies, but also affect both the quantity and quality of law reform.

Handling typical requests from these groups, for example, increases the quantity of reform litigation. Community organization requests vary depending on their goals and methods. Community development groups, for example, typically ask program lawyers to incorporate them, secure tax-exempt status, assist in planning activities, and help in securing grants. Advocacy groups, which constitute the majority of groups serviced by the program, ask lawyers to research specific areas of the law and analyze proposed and extant legislation and regulations. Community groups appearing at legislative hearings enlist lawyers to prepare testimony and accompany them. Groups employing direct-action tactics expect their lawyers to attend demonstrations to observe the legality of police behavior and "look official."[7] In general, advocacy groups expect program lawyers to be thoroughly informed about problems that affect them and assist in fashioning strategies to solve them. One veteran program lawyer explained:

> Community groups want people who are well informed about the area they're in. They need to know that I know the answers to a lot of things and can just say, "here's the answer to that." And they want a quick answer and they don't like to feel they know more than you do.

These requests combined with the development of skills needed to satisfy them increase the likelihood that program lawyers will engage in social reform activity. Problems brought to lawyers by community groups often involve broad policy questions requiring reform strategies for resolution. In contrast to individuals, who by and large seek solutions to problems affecting only themselves, organizations concern themselves with problems endemic to a poverty class. Representing groups, then, increases the probability that lawyers will handle policy-related cases, as evidenced in the comments of one Metro City Legal Services attorney:

Q. What differences do you see in representing individual clients and groups?

R. The difference is that you don't get the individual coming in saying, "I'm interested in a jobs program." They won't think of that as an individual. . . . Individuals as individuals do not take on major things or try to get things administered properly because they don't have the time to invest. That's what organizations are for. They'll come in and ask for advice about the jobs program.

To represent community organizations adequately, program lawyers devote a great deal of time to group work and develop an expertise in a substantive area. Substantive expertise enables lawyers to identify broad problems that lawyers without such knowledge are less able to identify. Thus, the expert knowledge program lawyers develop to better service their group clients serves to increase their chances of identifying issues requiring social reform strategies.

Community organization requests also affect the amount of reform work by focusing attorneys' attention on tasks which may lead to the discovery of unanticipated reform issues. Program lawyers discover reform issues that they would not have considered in the course of responding to specific groups' requests. This occurs because groups' requests typically involve research into broad, policy-relevant substantive areas. One attorney summarized this process:

Once we get involved with a group, we go to their meetings in the evening and develop personal relationships with these folks. It's a very fluid kind of thing. What'll happen, for example, is that the organization will get information that the gas company is about to propose a 30% rate hike. So they call us and say, "look, we need you to prepare testimony. We're going to testify before the rate commission and we need some testimony." In the process of preparing testimony you discover that there was some discrepancy in the way the rate was set last time. So you file a lawsuit in order to assure it doesn't happen again. It's a snowball.

The relationship between community groups and program lawyers not only increases lawyers' chances of handling policy suits, it also enhances its sophistication. Ongoing relations with community groups enable lawyers to devise and implement systematic strategies of reform, strategies most commonly employed by lawyers representing affluent, powerful, highly organized interests, such as business corporations.[8] Because they represent in courts what Marc Galanter refers to as "repeat players," Metro City Legal Services lawyers with the assistance of groups are able to shape entire substantive areas, such as welfare and employment law, so that they reflect the interests of the poor.

Also, program lawyers monitor the implementation of reform victories through their contacts with community organizations. For example, over the years program suits have established an elaborate set of procedural safeguards for public housing tenants. However, the safeguards had not been implemented properly by the Metro City Housing Authority. Through their contacts with community housing groups, program attorneys became aware of this problem and filed suit to place the Authority in receivership. One lawyer working on the case described the crucial role of community groups in monitoring the implementation of past reform victories:

I can think of three or four lawsuits I was involved in that developed procedural rights. Grievance hearings, for example. . . . People file their grievance hearing and win but nothing happens. We filed a grievance on behalf of the Metro City West Housing Group. We won. The Housing Authority did nothing. They came back to us and we went back to court and the court held the Housing Authority in contempt. They still didn't comply. So tenant groups say, "look, all these rights but I don't see the housing getting any better. There has to be a better approach." So we got together with those groups who were complaining and decided to sue for receivership.

Finally, and perhaps most significant, ongoing contacts with community groups affect the success of law reform activity. Novel legal theories are often the central elements in law reform litigation. However, these theories are frequently rejected by judges because of their novelty. Working with the same client groups year after year, much like corporate lawyers and their business clients, permits poverty lawyers in Metro City to present their arguments repeatedly in the hope that the judge's initial resistance will weaken and the merits eventually will be recognized.

This strategy, which program lawyers refer to as "educating judges," had been successful, for example, in the utility rate area. In 1969, program lawyers on behalf of several consumer groups challenged an electric company's rate increase approved by the state's Public Utility Commission. They argued unsuccessfully that the increase discriminated against low volume residential users who pay twice as much per kilowatt hour as commercial and industrial users. Attorneys argued this point repeatedly over the years until in 1978 the Public Utility Commission incorporated the logic into their decision. The Commission approved a 9 percent rate increase for commercial and industrial users and limited the increase to 3 percent for low volume residential users. When several corporations challenged the decision's constitutionality, Metro City Legal Services lawyers with their group clients intervened in the suit and successfully defended the decision.[9]

LOCAL DISSATISFACTION WITH PROGRAM OPERATIONS

Given the fact the Metro City Legal Services is surrounded by organizations with a diverse set of preferences, it is perhaps inevitable that its choice to ally with low-income groups and pursue law reform engenders opposition from other local organizations and individuals. The most significant sources of dissatisfaction with the program's operations are segments of the bar association, government agency lawyers, and the judiciary.

The Bar Association

Historically, the Metro City Bar Association has been divided in its support for the program. The bar leadership, composed primarily of lawyers from large corporate firms, assisted in establishing the program and supported it over the years. In contrast, small firm lawyers and solo practitioners opposed Metro City Legal Services from its inception.

When the OEO announced its intention in the 1960s to fund a legal services program in Metro City, several solo practitioners brought an unsuccessful lawsuit seeking to block its creation. When the bar association passes resolutions in support of continued funding for legal services, small firm lawyers and solo practitioners flood the local bar journal with letters of protest.

Private lawyers critical of the program voice a number of complaints about its lawyers. Many believe that program lawyers service ineligible clients and handle statutorily prohibited cases. Some criticize their methods of representation, arguing that program lawyers employ unfair and unethical tactics. For example, smaller practitioners allege that program lawyers consciously prolong losing cases, seeking to force settlements favorable to their clients. Finally, several local lawyers oppose the social reform activity of Metro City Legal Services attorneys. The brief comments of one solo practitioner provides some of the flavor of their views:

> There is a considerable amount of discontent among smaller practitioners like myself concerning this outfit. If you ask 100 smaller practitioners if MCLS takes business away from them, 98 would say yes. They use dilatory tactics to force your hand. They also use tax money to develop broad litigation tactics and have an advantage in seeing cases through to the bitter end.

In general, program lawyers recognize the importance of the bar's support for legal services funding, but many feel it inappropriate to cultivate their support. Indeed, very few program lawyers join the local bar and even fewer attend meetings and social gatherings. Many in the program believe that participating in bar association activities is tantamount to "selling out" and that good relations with private lawyers might result in the compromising of clients. As one attorney put it:

> It's important to me to be professionally respected, but I don't think MCLS should ever be in a position where the private bar likes us or is comfortable with us. We should be viewed as a necessary evil.

The distance program lawyers place between themselves and the private bar along with their aggressive representational style may have negative consequences for some of their clients. A few program attorneys report difficulties securing favors and courtesies from opposing counsel that private lawyers typically enjoy. They attribute their problems to the posture of other lawyers in the organization, as evidenced in the comments that follow:

> People here who don't give a damn about the private bar make life unnecessarily difficult. They're not being realistic because as lawyers we don't work in a vacuum. . . . I will have problems sometimes because lawyers have had a bad experience with a MCLS attorney. You know, if I call up another attorney as I did recently and say, "listen, I want to get this case continued because I want to get in contact with my client," they say, "no, I can't go along with you. You people in legal services are a pain in the ass. You never give me a break, so sorry."

Government Agency Lawyers

Of all the external groups with whom Metro City Legal Services lawyers interact, relations perhaps are most strained with attorneys representing government agencies. This is not surprising, given the fact that agency lawyers defend many of the institutions program lawyers and clients seek to reform. The animosity that many government lawyers feel toward program lawyers became evident prior to interviews when, during initial telephone conversations employed to schedule interviews, several complained openly about their activities, tactics, and personalities. During one interview, a government lawyer referred to notes he had prepared for our meeting. Regardless of the question asked, he read specific charges against the program listed in his notes.

Government lawyers voice several common complaints. Without exception, those interviewed feel that program staff are difficult to negotiate with and likely to offer unreasonable and unacceptable terms. As one government lawyer put it:

> I very rarely settle with MCLS. Their terms of settlement are outrageous. They will usually allow you to pick the day of the week that the department will commit suicide. I'm serious. The settlement terms are so ridiculous that you look at them and say, "if I lose in court, the odds are I'll get a better deal than if I settled. Why should I settle?"

Several factors account for the difficulties government lawyers experience in negotiating with program lawyers. First, the nature of issues litigated and remedies sought by the program often do not lend themselves to negotiations. The broad questions of public policy that Metro City Legal Services litigates often have no middle ground and their requests for broad-ranging remedies, such as mandatory injunctions and long-term consent decrees, are opposed by government agencies fearful of court involvement in their operations.

Further, negotiations are hindered because many of the suits filed against government agencies fall within the parameters of the Civil Rights Attorneys' Fees Act of 1976, legislation permitting court awarded fees when successful suits are brought involving civil rights issues.[10] Fees are sought and awarded not only when the court renders a judgment, but also when government lawyers accept the plaintiff's negotiating terms. One government lawyer explained:

> Once they bring a lawsuit it's very tough to change our position in response to that lawsuit because all of a sudden we become liable for attorneys' fees. So what it does is dig people into bargaining positions. Once litigation starts, you're dug into the position you're in even if you agree with and are willing to do what they want as a matter of substance.

Finally, successful negotiations are less likely in cases employing class action procedures and in those with an organizational plaintiff.[11] In these circumstances, program attorneys and their clients are interested in establishing broad principles of law and lawyers do not experience the intense client pressure to settle that is characteristic of individual plaintiffs. A government lawyer commented:

> In major litigation it is difficult to negotiate because they're not really representing a client. It's not like a private lawyer who has a client there in the office with a definable interest that is usually money.

Government lawyers also complain about the program's use of lawsuits to collect information not directly relevant to the immediate case. Many of the government lawyers who were interviewed reported that program lawyers spend a great deal of time and effort seeking to gain access to agency records and documents, a technique they felt is used to discover other litigable issues. Their concerns are illustrated in the comments that follow:

They will use excessive discovery. They're just notorious for endless deposition. Sometimes it seems like a fishing expedition, to find out more information. They can then use this information to develop other lawsuits.

The strained relations between program staff and agency lawyers may have adverse effects on Metro City's lawyers and clients. I uncovered some evidence in interviews with government lawyers suggesting that in certain circumstances agency lawyers employ their discretion in ways that may hurt the program's cause. For example, one government lawyer stated:

So much of the legal business in discretionary, never sees the light of day, never gets into any kind of document that ends up in court. And it's very hard . . . in fact, a couple of times I had the opportunity to exercise my discretion and just nail a MCLS attorney or a client of theirs. And I really try not to because that's lousy. But it's so hard when they've done their damnedest for the past two months to harass you and your client in court or made you answer abusive interrogatories just because the rules say you can't get out of it. It just strains the bounds of human nature not to.

The Local Judiciary

State court judges in Metro City support federally funded legal services. Without exception, those interviewed believe that Metro City Legal Services provides a needed service to indigents and that program lawyers are competent and committed. However, they express several criticisms. Family court judges, for example, charge that program attorneys are "too technical" and rigid in their advocacy. Several judges blame the program for court delay, charging that program attorneys use dilatory tactics as a weapon in negotiations and raise unnecessary issues on principle. All of the judges interviewed believe that program staff engage in too much social reform activity. One judge put it this way:

One of the things that's unfortunate about this group is that they're an elitist organization. They're primarily concerned with getting those cases that they could take up to the Court of Appeals or the Supreme Court so they could change social standards of law, if you will, and not so concerned with representing the individual who needed help with smaller problems. . . . I subscribe to the view that 80% of the lawyers over there should be doing the nuts and bolts work of representing clients.

Like solo practitioners, some Metro City judges felt that the program might represent ineligible clients. To monitor the program, the court held hearings on all requests to proceed *in forma pauperis*. Judges complain to the program director regarding client eligibility and the behavior of staff lawyers in their courtrooms. Those judges critical of the program's reform activity write letters to the program's director and the Legal Services Corporation. However, judges were unsuccessful and generally frustrated in their attempts to change the program's orientation, as the comments of one judge indicate:

> I'll call the director with any complaints I have. I've not been able to do much good with them, however. I think they bring too many class actions, but we've never been able to stop that.

While it is possible that the critical views of judges toward the program adversely affect their clients, program lawyers in general feel that they cannot adjust their representational style or strategies to conform to judges' preferences. One lawyer, describing the consequences to the program of seeking a writ of mandamus against a local judge, summarized this view:

> There was a transition period where maybe some of our clients didn't fare well in front of him. We don't make it explicit to every client, I suppose, but we try to make it clear that we will do everything for our clients, represent them with zeal. And they understand that this sometimes makes us unpopular. The clients that come to us appreciate that.

SUMMARY

The Metro City Legal Services case study illustrates some conditions under which reform-oriented lawyers may engage in legal activity that is more or less consistent with their personal preferences. Program policies and performance measures provide program staff with the incentive and time needed to engage in law reform. Equally important, lawyers' alliances with low-income groups promote law reform in a number of ways. Community groups assist lawyers in identifying problems and potential plaintiffs, help in designing law reform litigation, and improve its quality. In the course of responding to typical community group requests, lawyers uncover other potential reform issues. Further, community groups supply crucial political support, shielding the program from opposition from other external political actors. Thus, program policies and the nature of the local environment not only provide Metro City Legal Services lawyers with the freedom to pursue law reform, but in many ways they encourage it and enhance its sophistication.

The three chapters that follow seek to identify those factors which account for activity differences among the five programs studied. To begin, the next chapter assesses the influence of lawyers' personal characteristics on activity.

NOTES

1. On the decline of low-income advocacy groups, see Marilyn Gittell, *Limits to Citizen Participation: The Decline of Community Organizations* (Beverly Hills, California: Sage Publications, 1980).

2. For more detail on the sample, see Appendix B of this work.

3. This information is taken from the union contract I received from a program administrator.

4. See Robert G. Meadow and Carrie Menkel-Meadow, "The Origins of Political Commitment: Background Factors and Ideology Among Legal Services Attorneys," paper presented at the annual meeting of the Law and Society Association, Toronto, Canada, June 3, 1982; and Carol Ruth Silver, "The Imminent Failure of Legal Services for the Poor: Why and How to Limit Caseloads," *Journal of Urban Law* 46 (1969): pp. 217–248.

5. A new director, appointed several months before I began my field research, had stopped this practice.

6. The relations between neighborhood and central office lawyers in Metro City are similar to those described by Carlin in San Francisco Neighborhood Legal Assistance Foundation in the late 1960s. See Jerome E. Carlin, "Store Front Lawyers in San Francisco," *Trans-Action* 6 (April 1970): pp. 64–74.

7. One community organization leader commented on the reason for this request as follows: "When we've taken actions such as sit-ins, street blockings, and such, we've always managed to get one of the lawyers to come out and look official. Not that they really do anything, but when you have someone there that says I'm a lawyer it helps with the law."

8. On differences between representing organizations on an ongoing basis and representing individuals, see Marc Galanter, "Why the 'Haves' Come Out Ahead: Speculations on the Limits of Legal Change," *Law and Society Review* 9 (Fall 1974): pp. 95–160.

9. Even though program lawyers brought several successful law reform suits, a few cases that they "won" in court resulted in negative consequences for their clients. For example, the state's Department of Welfare had a program that provided low-income people under 21 years of age with free eye examinations and corrective lenses. An attorney challenged this program in court, arguing that the statute creating the program discriminated on the basis of age. The federal district court judge agreed, but because the welfare department did not have sufficient funds to examine and issue corrective lenses to all low-income people, the program was eliminated entirely. These types of law reform "victories" were rare. Even the most vocal critics of the program could cite only a handful of such cases.

10. For a discussion of the Civil Rights Attorneys' Fees Act of 1976, see E. R. Larson, "Civil Rights Attorneys' Fees Award Act of 1976," *Clearinghouse Review* 10 (January 1977): pp. 778–781; and Note, "Civil Rights Attorneys' Fees Act of 1976," *St. John's Law Review* 52 (Summer 1978): pp. 562–593.

11. On the dynamics of negotiations in class action litigation, see Note, "Developments in the Law—Class Action," *Harvard Law Review* 89 (May 1976): 1373–1383. For a discussion of differences between organizational and individual litigants, see Marc Galanter, "Why the 'Haves' Come Out Ahead."

6

THE LAWYERS

The case studies presented in Chapters 4 and 5 suggest that personal attributes of poverty lawyers have different effects on legal activity in two diverse programs. In the Suburban program, policies and the local environment constrained lawyers wishing to do law reform. In contrast, Metro City attorneys were free to engage in activity they preferred. This chapter broadens the scope of the analysis by comparing attributes of attorneys in five programs and offering a personal portrait of all legal services lawyers participating in the study. The comparative analysis seeks to uncover staff attributes that influence legal activity across the five programs and assist in explaining variation in mixes of law reform and service.

The following section begins the analysis by assessing the motivations of attorneys for accepting positions in poverty law programs. Subsequent sections examine lawyers' backgrounds, career ambitions, political identifications, ideologies, and attitudes.

MOTIVATIONS FOR LEGAL SERVICES WORK

Most attorneys in each of the five programs sought a legal services job because of their commitment to aid the poor. It is striking that out of 75 attorneys in the sample, only 14 (18 percent) accepted positions for other reasons, including opportunities for gaining legal experience, working in an informal environment, the program's location, and lack of other offers. But even though most lawyers claimed to have entered legal services for altruistic reasons, their motivations varied somewhat depending on the time period in which they attended law school.

Similar to the pattern found in Metro City Legal Services, attorneys attending law school in the 1960s and early 1970s were largely influenced by, and explicitly linked their career choice to, the political movements of the times. The civil rights movement and Vietnam War protests had a profound effect on most of the lawyers in this cohort. The comments of one Regional Rural attorney are typical of lawyers attending law school at this time.

> I came out of the 60s and I wanted to go to law school so that I could get the skills needed to promote some kind of social change. . . . I had spent some time in the anti-Vietnam movement and believed that one person could make a difference. It was the time of the War on Poverty, a war that I fully believed in. . . . So I wasn't interested in doing a lot of the things that people in law school are interested in. I wasn't interested in making a lot of money.

Attorneys attending law school more recently had less explicit political motivations for seeking legal services work. In general, this group felt some obligation to help the disadvantaged, at least for the first few years of their legal careers. However, unlike their older colleagues, they did not perceive their involvement in poverty law as part of larger social and political concerns. The remarks of a Rustic Legal Services lawyer illustrate the motivations of many younger lawyers.

> In law school I decided to do legal services work at least for awhile. I wanted to do what I could to see that the poor had their day in court. I felt an obligation . . . that this was the time to meet my professional responsibility.

Attorneys' motivations for working in legal services programs do not appear to be associated with the activity mixes in the five programs. Nearly all of the lawyers accepted their positions for altruistic reasons. Both those who connect their choice to broader political concerns and those who do not work in each of the five programs. The program engaging in the largest amount of law reform, Metro City Legal Services, employs more lawyers without political motivations than those with them. Further, Regional Rural Legal Ser-

Table 6
Age of Lawyers

Age	N	%
less than 30	23	(32)
30-35	38	(52)
36-40	9	(13)
over 40	2	(03)
Total	72	100

Mean = 31.8
Median = 31.0

vices, a program primarily engaging in service to individual clients, employs a majority of lawyers attracted to legal services for political reasons.

DEMOGRAPHIC AND BACKGROUND CHARACTERISTICS

The age distribution of attorneys in the present sample is shown in Table 6. The majority are between 30 and 35 years of age. A smaller but significant percentage (32 percent) are under 30. Few lawyers in the sample are over 36. On average, attorneys in the sample are 31 years old, the same average reported by Barbara A. Curran et al. for legal aid lawyers nationwide in 1980.[1]

Attorneys in this sample are more experienced than those surveyed by Handler et al. in 1967.[2] Forty percent of the legal services lawyers in their national sample had two years or less of legal experience, although 37 percent had been attorneys for seven years or more. Table 7 indicates the dramatic difference in experience between attorneys in my sample and the earlier group. While the percentage of veteran lawyers in the two samples is similar, only about 21 percent of attorneys in my sample are recent law school graduates. This may suggest that legal services lawyers have become more experienced since 1967, an interpretation consistent with Robert G. Meadow and Carrie Menkel-Meadow's findings from a 1981 sample of legal services lawyers in two programs.[3] In their sample, only 22 percent of the attorneys had two years or less of legal experience. Further, lawyers in my sample and those studied by Meadow and Menkel-

Table 7
Years of Legal Experience

Years		N	%
0-2		16	(21.3)
over 2-4		12	(16.0)
over 4-6		19	(25.3)
over 6		28	(37.3)
	Total	75	100 (rounded)

Mean = 5.0
Median = 5.5

Meadow had an average of five years of experience, considerably higher than that reported by Handler, et al.

Table 8 reports the type of undergraduate institution attended by lawyers in my sample. A plurality (47 percent) attended a public university. Nearly as many (42 percent) graduated from a private college or university. A small number, 8 of 74 or 11 percent, attended a prestigious private college or university.[4]

As shown in Table 9, only a small percentage of lawyers in my sample (16 percent) attended an elite or prestigious law school.[5] This finding corresponds to the earlier work of Handler et al., which reported that only 15 percent of legal services lawyers nationwide attended a major national law school.[6] Most of the lawyers in the 1967 sample and those in my group graduated from less distinguished state or private law schools.

Table 8
Type of Undergraduate School Attended

Type of Institution		N	%
Public		35	(47)
Private, non-prestige		31	(42)
Private, prestige[a]		8	(11)
	Total	74	100

[a]Harvard, Princeton, Yale, Williams, Wesleyan, Columbia, Dartmouth, Cornell, Penn, Brown, Stanford

Table 9
Type of Law School Attended

Type of Law School	N	%
Elite[a]	5	(07)
Prestigious[b]	7	(09)
State, non-prestige	29	(39)
Private, non-prestige	34	(45)
Total	75	100

[a]Harvard, Yale, Columbia, Chicago, Michigan, Stanford

[b]Berkeley, NYU, Penn, Virginia, UCLA, Cornell, Texas, Duke, Northwestern

Finally, Table 10 indicates where staff lawyers were born compared to their place of employment. The vast majority (66 percent) were born and raised outside the area where they practice law. Thirty-four percent were brought up in the area where they now practice.

Are these demographic and background characteristics associated with lawyers' legal activity? Do differences among lawyers in age, experience, education, and location of upbringing assist in explaining varying activity mixes among the five programs? Table 11 shows the distribution of these characteristics among programs and suggests some answers.

Metro City attorneys, on average, are slightly older (mean = 33 years) and possess more legal experience (mean = 6.7 years) than lawyers in the other four programs. This is beneficial to MCLS

Table 10
Location of Birth in Relation to Area of Employment

Location	N	%
Same Area	25	(34)
Outside Area	48	(66)
Total	73	100

lawyers wishing to engage in law reform. Veteran lawyers acquire the skills needed to engage in social reform work and are able to teach them to new recruits. Programs staffed primarily by recent law school graduates, like Rustic Legal Services, are less able to engage in a significant amount of law reform. The influence of legal experience on activity is illustrated by the comments of a MCLS and RLS attorney:

(MCLS): One of the most valuable resources we have in this program is our experience. We probably have at least 25 lawyers with at least 6 years experience, ranging up to 13 years or something in that neighborhood. That means that lawyers know how to handle the complex class action or whatever comes up.

(RLS): I've only been out of law school for about two years now. I'm still learning how to handle the routine stuff. I just think it's banging my head against the wall to attack a statute because of my inexperience. I don't know how to attack it.

The explanatory importance of age and legal experience should not be overstated. On average, attorneys in Industrial Region Legal Services, Suburban Legal Services, and Regional Rural Legal Services are over 30 years of age and have approximately five years of legal experience. Thus, although age and experience assist legal services lawyers in pursuing social reform, they do not ensure that a substantial amount of time will be allocated to it.

Lawyers' educational backgrounds vary among programs. The most striking finding is that Metro City attorneys attended prestigious undergraduate institutions and elite or prestigious law schools to a much greater extent than lawyers in the other programs. Six of 25 MCLS respondents, or 24 percent of the sample, attended a prestigious undergraduate school compared to only two other lawyers in the remaining programs. Nearly 50 percent of MCLS lawyers attended either an elite or prestigious law school while no lawyer in the other programs did so.

Though at first educational background appears crucial for explaining activities, further analysis suggests it is not. Some Metro City attorneys with elite educational backgrounds do not engage in much or any law reform and some of the most active law reformers do not have distinguished academic backgrounds. Five of the MCLS

Table 11
Selected Demographic and Background Characteristics by Program

	Program						
	MCLS		IRLS		SLS	ReqRLS	RLS
	N	%	N	%	N	N	N
Demographic:							
Age							
less than 30	5	(21)	8	(30)	3	4	3
30-35	14	(58)	16	(59)	4	3	1
36-40	5	(21)	2	(7)	2	1	0
over 40	0	(0)	1	(4)	0	1	0
	24	(100)	27	(100)	9	9	4
Mean	33		31.7		32	31	28.5
Median	32		31.0		32	31	29.0
Background:							
Years legal experience							
0-2	1	(4)	6	(21)	3	3	3
over 2-4	5	(20)	6	(21)	1	0	0
over 4-6	5	(20)	10	(36)	2	2	0
over 6	14	(56)	6	(21)	3	4	1
	25	(100)	28	(99)	9	9	4
Mean	6.7		5		4.9	5.3	3.5
Median	7.0		5		5.0	5.5	2.0
Type of Undergraduate School Attended							
Public	9	(36)	15	(56)	3	6	2
Private, non-prestige	10	(40)	12	(44)	5	2	2
Private, prestige	6	(24)	0	(0)	1	1	0
	25	(100)	27	(100)	9	9	4
Type of Law School Attended							
Elite	5	(20)	0	(0)	0	0	0
Prestigious	7	(28)	0	(0)	0	0	0
State, non-prestige	9	(36)	14	(50)	1	4	1
Private, non-prestige	4	(16)	14	(50)	8	5	3
	25	(100)	28	(100)	9	9	4
Location of Birth in Relation to Area of Employment							
Same area	6	(25)	13	(48)	4	0	2
Outside area	18	(75)	14	(52)	5	9	2
	24	(100)	27	(100)	9	9	4

lawyers who attended distinguished law schools spend nearly 50 percent of their time on law reform. But five others spend between 20 percent and 40 percent of their time on law reform and two others spend 10 percent or less. Of the eight others with less distinguished educational backgrounds for whom data was collected, six spend 50 percent or more of their time on law reform and two spend 10 percent or less. Further, IRLS lawyers without distinguished educational backgrounds spend some of their time pursuing reform.

Where staff lawyers were brought up varies among agencies, but was not associated with program activity. Regional Rural Legal Services is staffed exclusively by lawyers born and raised outside the area. The other programs include a mix of hometown and "immigrant" attorneys. MCLS has the second largest percentage of lawyers born outside the area, 75 percent (18 of 24), but IRLS, SLS, and RLS also employ a significant number.

The lack of association between lawyers' backgrounds and legal activity is consistent with Handler et al.'s earlier work on OEO attorneys. Although they found an association between a few background characteristics and activity (class standing, father's political stance, parents' involvement in social reform organizations), together they only accounted for 5 percent of the variance in percentage of time spent on law reform work.[7] More generally, these findings are consistent with studies that fail to find strong relationships between social backgrounds and the behavior of other legal actors, such as judges.[8]

CAREER AMBITIONS

A majority of attorneys in my sample did not view their involvement in legal services as a steppingstone to other careers or areas of law practice. As Table 12 indicates, over half hoped to remain in legal services. Approximately another third intended to move from legal services to private practice, with most of these lawyers (88 percent) hoping to remain in the county in which they presently practiced.

Table 13 shows some dramatic differences among the five programs in lawyers' ambitions and suggests that ambition may influence activity in four of them. Only 9 percent (2 of 23) of Metro City attorneys desire to enter private practice, while 70 percent (16 of 23)

Table 12
Career Ambitions

Ambition	N	%
Remain in legal services	40	(53.3)
Other public interest law	3	(04.0)
Government legal work	1	(01.3)
Teaching	2	(02.7)
Private practice -- same county	23	(30.7)
Private practice -- other county	3	(04.0)
Politics	1	(01.3)
Unsure	2	(02.7)
	75	100

intend to follow a career in poverty law. In contrast, 50 percent (15 of 30) of Industrial Region attorneys, 3 of 9 in Suburban Legal Services, and 3 of 4 in Rustic Legal Services hope to enter private practice in their local communities. A smaller percentage of attorneys in each of these programs intend to follow a poverty law career—11 of 30 (34 percent) in IRLS, 5 of 9 in SLS, and only 1 of 4 in RLS.

Attorneys intending to enter private practice in the local community tend to be wary of the legal community's reaction to their work.[9] Bar association leaders, private practitioners, and judges interviewed for this study opposed law reform, an important constraint on lawyers depending on positive evaluations from these sources for career advancement.[10]

In Regional Rural Legal Services, ambitions do not relate to activities. The distribution of lawyers' career ambitions is similar to that in Metro City. Most attorneys (7 of 9) intend to remain in legal services. None hope to enter private practice in their community.[11] So, while the presence of a large proportion of lawyers intending to follow a poverty law career and the absence of attorneys seeking to enter private practice eliminates one obstacle to law reform, these conditions do not guarantee that programs will pursue it.

PARTISAN IDENTIFICATION, IDEOLOGY, AND ATTITUDES

The distribution of lawyers' partisan identifications are displayed in Table 14.[12] Nearly one-half (48 percent) identify with the Dem-

Table 13
Career Ambitions by Program

Ambition	Program						
	MCLS		IRLS		SLS	RLS	RegRLS
	N	%	N	%	N	N	N
Stay with legal services	16	(70)	11	(34)	5	1	7
Other public interest law	2	(9)	1	(4)	0	0	0
Government legal work	1	(4)	0	(0)	0	0	0
Teaching	1	(4)	0	(0)	0	0	1
Private practice-same county	2	(9)	15	(50)	3	3	0
Private practice-other county	0	(0)	1	(4)	1	0	1
Politics	1	(4)	0	(0)	0	0	0
Unsure	0	(0)	2	(8)	0	0	0
	23	(100)	30	(100)	9	4	9

ocratic Party. Another one third (33 percent) are Independents. Only 5 of 73, or 7 percent, of the attorneys responding to this question identify with the Republican Party.

As Table 15 indicates, attorneys' partisan identifications vary among programs. But differences in party identification do not appear to be associated with varying activity mixes. Lawyers in programs with very different mixes of law reform and service—MCLS, IRLS, RLS, and RegRLS—describe themselves primarily as Dem-

Table 14
Partisan Identification

Party	N	%
Democrat	35	(48)
Republican	5	(07)
Independent	24	(33)
Other	9	(12)
	73	100

Table 15
Partisan Identification by Program

Party	Program						
	MCLS		IRLS		SLS	RegRLS	RLS
	N	%	N	%	N	N	N
Democrat	9	(38)	15	(55)	3	5	3
Republican	0	(0)	1	(4)	4	0	0
Independent	11	(46)	7	(26)	2	3	1
Other	4	(16)	4	(15)	0	1	0
	24	100	27	100	9	9	4

ocrats or as Independents. In Metro City, a slightly larger proportion of attorneys are Independents, while in Industrial Region and the rural programs more lawyers identify with the Democratic Party. In Suburban Legal Services, the modal identification is with the Republican Party, but if we combine categories a majority identify themselves as Democrats and Independents.

Table 16 shows that attorneys' political ideology tends to fall to the left of the spectrum.[13] The plurality of lawyers (45 percent) characterize their political beliefs as left-of-liberal. A slightly smaller percentage (38 percent) view their ideology as liberal. Only 11 of 72 attorneys, or 15 percent, characterize their political views as moderate or conservative.

Table 17 compares lawyers' ideology among the five programs and shows that it varies only slightly. Metro City and Regional Rural employ the largest proportion of attorneys with left-of-liberal attitudes—13 of 23 MCLS lawyers (57 percent) and 6 of 9 in RegRLS.

Table 16
Political Ideology

Ideology	N	%
Conservative	3	(04)
Moderate	8	(11)
Liberal	27	(38)
Left of liberal	34	(47)
	72	100

Table 17
Political Ideology by Program

Ideology	Program						
	MCLS		IRLS		SLS	RegRLS	RLS
	N	%	N	%	N	N	N
Conservative	1	(4)	1	(4)	1	0	0
Moderate	2	(9)	4	(15)	1	1	0
Liberal	7	(30)	10	(37)	5	2	3
Left of liberal	13	(57)	12	(44)	2	6	1
	23	100	27	100	9	9	4

A slightly smaller percentage (44 percent) of Industrial Region attorneys characterize their ideology as left-of-liberal and only 2 of 9 in Suburban and 1 of 4 in Rustic do so.

Combining the liberal and left-of-liberal categories produces much less variation among programs. All lawyers in RLS, 8 of 9 in RegRLS, and 7 of 9 in SLS characterize their ideology as left-of-center. In the metropolitan programs, 20 of 23 MCLS attorneys (87 percent) and a slightly lower percentage of IRLS lawyers, 22 of 27 or 81 percent, hold left-of-center political values. Based on these data, a strong, direct link between ideology and program activity does not appear to exist.

As Table 18 shows, attorneys are divided regarding the appropriate mix of program activity.[14] A slight plurality (35 percent) believe that legal services programs should devote most, if not all, of their resources to servicing individual clients. Nearly one-third advocate law reform over service. Another third believe that legal services programs should divide their resources equally between service and reform.

Attorneys gave various reasons for preferring one set of activities over another. For some advocating service, their preference is linked to a traditional conception of the lawyer's role. According to these attorneys, the lawyer's primary function is to represent individuals with a variety of legal problems, not to seek, first and foremost, legal or social reform. Comments of a Suburban Legal Services attorney provide some of this perspective's flavor:

> We are lawyers. We have been trained in law school as lawyers. And lawyers represent individuals who come to them with problems. They don't try to

Table 18
Attitudes Regarding Appropriate Mix of Activity

Attitude	N	%	
Service orientation	26	(35.1)	
Reform orientation	24	(32.4)	
Equal mix	24	(32.4)	
	74	100	(rounded)

change the world. I believe that we ought to conduct ourselves as lawyers which means representing individual clients with whatever problems they may bring.

Many of these same attorneys oppose law reform because of its perceived consequences for individual clients. For example, several were critical of programs that do too much law reform, believing that it inevitably leads to excluding entire case categories and refusing to serve individual clients with routine legal problems. One Rustic lawyer explained:

I think that if you hope to be the poor people's law firm you should not keep your doors closed. You should, in fact, perform as any private attorney would and provide a full range of legal services to them. If you do too much of the law reform that means that some clients will not see an attorney. I just can't justify that.

In sharp contrast to the traditional role conceptions of lawyers advocating service, many who prefer reform view their role in political terms. They perceive themselves as representing an entire economic class and believe that legal services lawyers through their activities should seek to alter existing economic and power inequalities. As one Metro City attorney put it:

I guess I would summarize my philosophy of legal services as being one that . . . it's not original to me . . . but my notion is that lawyers and paralegals can serve as a means to help poor people become empowered by helping them to exercise latent powers and access to decisionmaking that the system affords them. . . . What I think we should really be about is shifting power to poor people. That requires different kinds of strategies. In devising a mix of impact stuff and individual stuff, I lean toward the impact stuff.

Several of these lawyers also link their preference for reform to their conception of the LSC's mission. They are aware of the OEO program's commitment to social reform and believe that LSC attorneys have a responsibility to continue in that tradition. For example, one Industrial Region lawyer observed:

We were born out of the War on Poverty and should seek as best we can to alleviate the institutional problems facing the poor. Poor people need individual representation, but individual representation is like spitting into the ocean if you really can't change the overall problem, the broader problem.

Attorneys preferring service and reform differed in their judgments regarding which set of activities most efficiently and effectively allocate scarce resources. Several of those preferring service are skeptical about law reform's effectiveness. Arguing that meaningful change cannot be achieved through the legal system, they believe that serving individual clients is the most effective means by which to assist the poor. The comments of a Rustic Legal Services attorney illustrate this view.

The 100 hours you spend trying to reform some institution or law isn't nearly as effective as helping the individual. I just think we can accomplish a lot more if we spend our time with individuals. I don't think you can get as much done attacking institutions. Our legal system just isn't structured for it.

But many lawyers preferring reform felt it was the most efficient use of scarce resources. To these attorneys, one important feature of test cases and class action suits is that a single successful action makes it unnecessary to bring several on behalf of individual clients. In the words of one Metro City lawyer:

I think it saves you a lot of the band-aid work, a lot of the individual representation work, if you handle the impact work correctly. And that includes not only litigation, but I think also a lot of the community education, and even though those days are over, community organizing. I think the more work you do on a large scale, the less you're going to have to do individual representation.

A few lawyers preferring service expressed concern about political repercussions of engaging in social reform activity. In discussing two of IRLS's most visible law reform suits, one that sought to merge two school districts for purposes of racial integration and the other challenging fares charged by the county transportation authority, one Industrial Region attorney argued:

I believe that we as legal services lawyers should devote our time to individual clients. I think there's often the tendency to jump into impact litigation too quickly. I think it should be discussed very carefully with many people before you decide a whole program should jump in and get involved with a particular issue. . . . When you're getting into things like the school desegregation case and the suit against the transportation authority downtown, then you're biting the hand that feeds you. I think that merging the ____ and ______ school districts was stupid to begin with because they had to know that they were gonna get all the resistance in the world from important people around the county. Sometimes people around here are just too impact litigation-minded.

While lawyers preferring law reform acknowledged that such activity generates opposition from those in positions of power, they believed that legal services lawyers should not permit political controversy or sanctions against their programs to influence their activity. Many of these attorneys cited professional codes of ethics as prohibiting lawyers from considering political reactions when designing strategies of representation. According to an Industrial Region lawyer:

Sure it's possible that you might get your head clubbed for filing some of those cases. Sure you get people angry with you. But the Code of Professional Responsibility says you represent your clients with zeal. If that means you upset some people, even some important people, then that's the way you have to go. And you can't let some political flack get in the way.

By and large, attorneys advocating an equal mix of reform and service did not provide philosophical or policy arguments in support. They simply argued that both types of activity are important and that programs should seek a balance. For example, one Rustic Legal Services lawyer remarked:

I really have no qualms with legal services being law reform minded. I think the system needs reform. But I think it's important as well to help people

Table 19
Attitudes Regarding Appropriate Mix of Activity by Program

Attitude	Program						
	MCLS		IRLS		SLS	RegRLS	RLS
	N	%	N	%	N	N	N
Service orientation	3	(12)	15	(56)	4	2	2
Reform orientation	14	(56)	6	(22)	2	2	0
Equal mix	8	(32)	6	(22)	3	5	2
	25	100	27	100	9	9	4

with their day to day problems. So I guess I fall somewhere in the middle. We should do both.

Table 19 shows that lawyers' views regarding appropriate activities vary among the five programs but do not appear to be associated with actual activity mixes. Fourteen of 25 (56 percent) Metro City attorneys advocate law reform over service. But 11 others (44 percent) believe that at least half of the program's resources should be allocated to service. In Industrial Region, the numbers are reversed. Fifteen of 27 lawyers (56 percent) advocate service over reform and 12 others (44 percent) believe that at least half of their resources should be directed toward social reform. Data from the metropolitan programs, then, suggest a relationship between attitudes and activity. However, lawyers' views in Suburban, Regional Rural, and Rustic do not conform to their activity mixes. A majority of SLS and RegRLS attorneys and 2 of 4 in RLS believe that resources allocated to social reform activity should at least equal those apportioned to service.

In three programs, there appears to be an association between program policymaker attitudes and activity. Policy decisions in Metro City are shared by an executive director and an employee union. The union, as shown in Tables 17 and 19, is staffed by a majority of lawyers with left-of-center, reformist attitudes, while the director characterizes his ideology as conservative and prefers service to law reform. But Metro City attorneys, through their union, participate in most decisions affecting activities and their activity mix more or less conforms to their personal preferences. In Suburban Legal Services, the director holds moderate political attitudes and prefers service to law reform. And even though the director of Rustic Legal Services considers himself a liberal, he advocates service over law reform.

But in two programs, Industrial Region and Regional Rural, management attitudes do not correspond directly with attitudes. Although the director of IRLS and administrators in RegRLS hold left-of-center political values and prefer an equal mix of service and social reform activity, lawyers in these programs do not distribute their time evenly between service and law reform.

The absence of a direct link between attitudes, ideology, and program activity is significant, given the assumption among many conservatives that legal services programs are staffed primarily by leftist attorneys whose behavior is guided by political ideology. Even though the data indicate a liberal orientation among legal services lawyers, they fail to suggest a simple association between personal predilection and behavior. Programs staffed by left-of-center, reformist attorneys do not necessarily allocate much of their time to law reform.[15]

SUMMARY

To summarize, data collected from attorneys in the five programs suggest that personal backgrounds, ambitions, and values do not explain differences in activity. None of the lawyers' characteristics examined exert a strong direct influence on program activity. Some assist lawyers and programs wishing to engage in law reform. Programs with a large proportion of attorneys experienced in law reform and without ambitions to enter private practice in the local community are aided in their pursuit of social reform. But these features only provide the opportunity for reform activity, they do not guarantee it.

The failure of the individual-level perspective to explain program activity raises important questions about the most common charges levied against the Legal Services Corporation by conservative critics. While it appears that legal services attorneys do indeed exhibit a liberal orientation in their political views, their political values do not translate necessarily into legal activity that seeks basic changes in American society.

NOTES

1. See Barbara A. Curran, Katherine J. Rosich, Clara N. Carson, and Mark C. Puccetti, *The Lawyer Statistical Report: A Statistical Profile of the U.S. Legal Profession in the 1980s* (Chicago, Illinois: American Bar Foundation, 1985), pp. 22–23.

2. Joel F. Handler, Ellen Jane Hollingsworth, and Howard S. Erlanger, *Lawyers and the Pursuit of Legal Rights* (New York: Academic Press, 1978), pp. 136–137. My sample of attorneys is neither national nor random. Comparisons between lawyers in my sample and the national sample are drawn for the purpose of suggesting possible trends, rather than providing conclusive evidence of them.

3. Robert G. Meadow and Carrie Menkel-Meadow, "The Origins of Political Commitment: Background Factors and Ideology Among Legal Services Attorneys," paper presented at the annual meeting of the Law and Society Association, Toronto, Canada, June 3, 1982, p. 10.

4. Of course, it is somewhat arbitrary to categorize certain institutions as "prestigious." I have used a standard list of institutions considered to be of the highest quality in other social science research.

5. Elite law schools are those most commonly cited among the top five in the country. Prestigious law schools are those rated consistently in the top fifteen, but not among the top five. The placement of institutions into these categories may be validated by examining ratings in Elliot M. Epstein, Jerome Shostak, and Lawrence M. Troy, *Barrons' Guide to Law School* (Woodbury, New York: Barron's Educational Series, Inc., 1980). The distinction between elite and prestigious law schools is used and discussed in John P. Heinz and Edward 0. Laumann, *Chicago Lawyers: The Social Structure of the Bar* (New York: Russell Sage Foundation and American Bar Foundation, 1982).

6. Handler et al., *Lawyers and the Pursuit of Legal Rights*, pp. 142–143.

7. Ibid., p. 148.

8. See the discussion of judicial background research in Jerome R. Corsi, *Judicial Politics: An Introduction* (Englewood Cliffs, New Jersey: Prentice-Hall, Inc., 1984), pp. 263–265.

9. On the influence of career ambitions on poverty lawyer behavior, see Jack Katz, *Poor People's Lawyers in Transition* (New Brunswick, New Jersey: Rutgers University Press, 1982).

10. Because of their ambitions to practice privately, lawyers depended

on the local legal community for what they perceived as "critical resources." For these attorneys, the legal community occupied an important place in the enacted environment. A more detailed discussion of the constraints imposed by the legal community on lawyer activity can be found in Chapter 8.

11. RegRLS lawyers noted that their community had an overabundance of lawyers practicing privately. Even if they hoped to enter private practice, their prospects for financial survival were not good. But when asked if their ambitions might change with a more receptive local market, all seven responded that it would not.

12. The four categories of partisan identification were collapsed from eight which appeared in the questionnaire. For each party, categories of strong, moderate, and weak identification were combined for a clearer, more efficient presentation.

13. The four categories of ideology were collapsed from six which appeared in the questionnaire. Those viewing themselves as "moderate conservatives" were combined with "conservatives" and "left liberals" were combined with "left radicals" into a "left-of-liberal" category.

14. During interviews, attorneys were asked about their beliefs regarding appropriate activity mixes for legal services programs. Responses favoring more service than reform were coded as "service orientation." Those favoring more law reform than service were coded as "reform orientation." Finally, those advocating an equal amount of each were coded as "equal mix."

15. Meadow and Menkel-Meadow also found no direct relationship between lawyer ideology and law reform activity in the two programs they studied. See Meadow and Menkel-Meadow, "The Origins of Political Commitment."

7

THE ORGANIZATIONAL CONTEXT

That personal attributes of poverty lawyers do not adequately explain their legal activity may be a function of the organizational setting in which they work. Legal services lawyers work in and are members of local, state, and national social service organizations; organizational memberships that may render it difficult to make truly independent decisions that correspond to personal beliefs. Indeed, organizational theorists have recognized for some time that organizations inculcate their own values and "decisional premises" to members that may override and even replace personal values.[1] Even if members do not internalize the organization's goals and values, its rules, practices, and standard operating procedures may constrain members.

This chapter explores the organizational context in which legal services attorneys work. What effect do organizational features of legal services programs have on the legal activity of their staff? To what extent do organizational rules and practices constrain poverty lawyers? The following section examines differences in program structure and some general operating features. Subsequent sections assess a variety of program policies and practices.

STRUCTURE AND GENERAL OPERATING FEATURES

There are significant differences in the administrative structure employed by the five programs. Administrative authority in Metro

Table 20
Administrative Structure by Program

	Program				
	MCLS	IRLS	SLS	RegRLS	RLS
Degree of centralization	low	high	high	low	high

City and Regional Rural is much more decentralized than in the other three programs. Decisionmaking authority in MCLS is distributed among several parties—an executive director, an employee union, and staff in individual offices. Attorneys in the several offices have nearly unlimited discretion in choosing cases and legal strategy. In RegRLS, a management committee composed of administrative attorneys from each of its three offices monitors program operations and serves as liaison to the board of directors, funding sources, and other external groups. But the committee provides little central direction to individual offices and, as a result, offices vary dramatically in the types of cases they handle and other operating features.

In sharp contrast, administrative authority in the other three programs is centralized. In two of the smaller programs, Suburban and Rustic, an executive director makes all important administrative decisions and directs daily operations. In Industrial Region, a few top administrators perform the same functions as the directors of SLS and RLS. Differences in administrative structure among the programs are summarized in Table 20.

General operating features of the programs also differ significantly. For example, Table 21 shows that the degree of attorney specialization varies among programs and suggests that it may affect the activity mix. Each lawyer in Metro City handles cases in a single substantive area. In contrast, lawyers in Suburban and Rustic are generalists.[2] A few central office specialists in Industrial Region bring reform litigation, while generalists in neighborhood offices primarily handle service cases. Finally, in Regional Rural, attorneys with varying degrees of specialization in two of its offices bring occasional law reform suits, and generalists in a third office engage solely in service

Table 21
Attorney Specialization by Program

	Program				
	MCLS	IRLS	SLS	RegRLS	RLS
Degree of specialization	high	mixed	low	mixed	low

activity.[3] This suggests that specialization has important consequences for the amount of law reform brought by attorneys. Lawyers who specialize seem to have more opportunities to engage in law reform because they interview clients with problems in only one substantive area. Specialized lawyers may more readily look across cases for patterns and issues. Further, specialization concentrates the lawyer's energies and avoids the distraction and fatigue associated with constant shifting of attention.

As Table 22 indicates, programs vary in the number of cases handled by staff lawyers.[4] Metro City lawyers have the lightest caseloads, facilitating their involvement in reform activity. Attorneys in the other programs struggle with heavy caseloads and cannot expend the resources necessary to engage in a substantial amount of time-consuming law reform. This suggests that left critics of legal services programs have correctly identified one important constraint on law reform activity—the size of attorney caseloads. The remarks of two lawyers, one from IRLS and the other from Regional Rural, summarize the feelings expressed by many lawyers in IRLS, SLS, RLS, and RegRLS and illustrate constraints imposed by heavy caseloads on social reform activity.

(IRLS): Even if I'd recognize something as an important issue, I hope it goes away because I don't have the time. I'm aware of it. I know I do it and know others do it too. You just fail to pursue something. You can always make a case into a big deal, but the problem is that we don't often have the time.

(RegRLS): Sometimes when there is a case that there are four or five things you can do for a client, you make adjustments based on your workload. At the top is something like major litigation to deal with a truth-in-lending

Table 22
Caseload Size by Program

	Program				
	MCLS	IRLS	SLS	ReqRLS	RLS
Caseload size	mixed, low-mod (majority moderate)	mixed, low-high (majority high)	high	mixed, mod-high (majority high)	high

problem that may be broadly felt. At the bottom is getting a quick disposition without going to court. There is a tendency, when you're packed with cases, to do only the fifth thing and not the first.

Heavy caseloads not only constrain law reform activity, but several lawyers felt they may adversely affect their preparation of individual service cases. As two lawyers from RLS put it:

The tremendous caseload I have will affect my work, sure. I always feel that there's more that I could do in any case. I always have the fear that there's this one case that I just didn't bother to look up this time because I had to go to somebody's hearing.

There are times when I feel totally overwhelmed. I've felt that I simply had too much to do and therefore I wasn't able to spend as much time preparing a case as I should.

PROGRAM POLICIES

Administrative policies governing the activity of program staff vary among programs. Table 23 summarizes differences in four sets of policies. The size of attorney caseloads is shaped by two sets of discretionary policies, case category exclusions and caseload adjustment. As Chapter 5 described, Metro City excludes a number of case categories that seldom involve law reform issues, such as divorce, wills, and name changes. Further, a caseload adjustment policy permits Metro City staff to remove themselves from client intake when overburdened with cases or when law reform efforts consume large portions of their time.

Table 23
Policies by Program

Policies	Program				
	MCLS	IRLS	SLS	RegRLS	RLS
Number caseload exclusions	high, fluctuating	low, stable	low, stable	mixed, fluctuating	low, stable
Caseload adjustment	yes	no	no	yes	no
Reform constraints	no	yes, indirect	yes, direct	yes, indirect	yes, direct
Performance measures	yes, reform	yes, service	no	no	no

Program policies in Rustic Legal Services, like those described in Chapter 4 for Suburban, require attorneys to handle large service caseloads. They exclude few case categories and prohibit attorneys from removing themselves from client intake for any reason. These policies are the same in all but one Industrial Region office, where a small staff of central office lawyers sees fewer clients than those in neighborhood offices, and manages caseloads light enough to permit involvement in law reform. Similarly, policies in two Regional Rural offices permit lawyers to engage in law reform. Several case categories are excluded and attorneys may adjust caseloads. But in both IRLS and RegRLS, attorneys employ these policies for purposes of engaging in social reform activity much less frequently than in Metro City. Thus, while left critics of legal services programs correctly identify one important constraint on law reform—large caseloads—policies that seek to free the lawyer's time do not ensure a substantial amount of reform activity.

Unlike attorneys in the other programs, Metro City lawyers are not deterred from pursuing social reform either directly or indirectly by program administrators. Because the program is so decentralized, composed of several virtually autonomous offices, staff have nearly unlimited discretion in filing class action suits and test cases. As one Metro City lawyer explained:

> We don't have people looking over our shoulders here telling us that this case shouldn't be brought and that that case is a loser. We don't have people supervising us to any great extent. Some people complain about it, but it gives you the freedom to do what you feel is best. . . . And you don't find anyone in this program asking that you drop some case because it's too hot. Maybe we need a bit of that, but the program has never shied away from anything to any great extent.

Administrators in Industrial Region and Regional Rural do not explicitly prohibit the filing of reform cases, but neither do they actively support such efforts. In IRLS neighborhood lawyers are required to handle a normal service caseload whether or not they are handling law reform cases. Difficulties in simultaneously handling both types of cases provide a powerful disincentive to lawyers contemplating involvement in reform litigation. Administrators in RegRLS also fail to encourage law reform by providing support to lawyers engaged in time-consuming cases. To engage in reform litigation, attorneys must choose reform cases carefully and convince office administrators to exclude other cases for a period of time. While RegRLS lawyers are able, on occasion, to persuade administrators to grant relief, the lack of consistent support decreases the amount of reform activity. The comments of one IRLS and one RegRLS attorney demonstrate the indirect constraints imposed by administrators on reform litigation:

(IRLS): Because of the caseloads here, people in the neighborhoods are pushed to get rid of their cases and not find issues. . . . If you find one, it means a hell of a lot of work for you and there's no compensation for it. It's not that the rest of your office takes over some of your cases.

(RegRLS): Although people say you're welcome to do as much impact litigation as you can, the emphasis has always been on service and you find it difficult to make the shift. They'll stand on the sidelines and cheer you on, but other than that they'll not provide the kinds of assistance necessary.

The director in Rustic Legal Services operates much like the director of Suburban Legal Services described in Chapter 4. Direct controls are employed to prohibit staff from filing class action suits, test cases, and actions that may generate controversy. The director of RLS described his approach:

I've certainly told my staff on occasion to be careful not to stir the waters. Sometimes it does more harm than good. I've always had the attitude that there's no sense going in with the idea of stirring up the water. You don't go in and just make waves. There's no sense in doing that because you'll create animosity, especially in a real conservative-type place like this.

The two metropolitan programs employ performance measures affecting activity. As discussed in Chapter 5, Metro City administrators for many years encouraged law reform by requesting from staff lists of reform victories and lawsuits in progress. In contrast, performance measures in Industrial Region encourage service activity. Offices within the program receive important resources, such as additional equipment and staff, based on the number of clients they serve. Offices serving the largest number of clients are rewarded, forcing each office to play what lawyers throughout the program refer to as the "numbers game." Two veteran IRLS lawyers described the significance of client numbers:

> When the resources in the program overall dwindle and the director has to start allocating attorneys and transferring attorneys, one thing he looks at is numbers. How many clients is this office servicing? Well, if this office is servicing 2000 clients a month and another office is seeing 1000 a month, then the 2000 office needs twice as many attorneys. So if you keep your numbers up or if your per capita client statistics are higher, then you're more likely to get more staff. You're going to get more support staff and more attorneys. So there's that pressure.

> Managing attorneys fight about their numbers. We call it the numbers game. Not just attorneys, but the number of secretaries you have is determined by how many clients you see. It seems kind of silly, but it makes a difference.

The number of clients served by lawyers and offices is also an important measure of performance among IRLS staff lawyers. By and large, attorneys view those handling the greatest number of cases as the most skilled lawyers in the program and compete among themselves over caseload numbers. Indeed, it appears that handling large quantities of cases in IRLS displaced the program's original goals of providing quality legal services or reforming laws and institutions.[5] "Goal displacement" in IRLS is evidenced in the remarks of two veteran staff lawyers:

> In this program, the original idea was not to get large numbers of clients for the sake of numbers. I think the emphasis on numbers came from a legitimate desire to create a program where you served as many people as you could. Unfortunately, we lost sight of where the saturation point was. When I started, the guy next to me was handling 150 cases and as a law student I had 50 to 60 cases. You just had them. They were there. I don't think it was a conscious desire to see how many cases you could get. I think it was an attitude that if you weren't seeing a lot of people, if you weren't handling a lot of cases, if you weren't reaching the point where you had to stay at night, you just weren't doing an adequate job.

> In this kind of business, you don't worry about how much money somebody's making. We don't charge for services, so we don't look at how much an office is bringing in. For a lack of anything else to compete about, we compete about the number of clients we see. It's an indication, I guess, of the success of the office. Rather than money, it's people.

The emphasis on client numbers in IRLS is illustrated further by the views of many neighborhood lawyers toward one central office attorney who brought a major reform lawsuit against the county jail. This lawyer spent nearly all of his time for a year preparing the case. Outraged that an attorney could devote so much time to one legal action, neighborhood lawyers began to refer to him sarcastically as "One Case." After he won the lawsuit, however, neighborhood lawyers showed more respect for him and his ability, as shown in the descriptions of these events by the lawyer involved in the lawsuit and a veteran neighborhood attorney:

> The issues in this case were enormous and many hadn't been litigated before. So this could have been perhaps 15 to 20 lawsuits. But of course it was perceived by the neighborhoods as one case. And they couldn't understand why I was working on one case for a year. Nobody here could understand because the mentality here is one case means a week or two. It certainly doesn't mean the better part of a year. So there was a lot of grumbling about this, and a great deal of ill feeling. People would come up to me and say, "How are you doing, One Case?" They'd say it in a humorous fashion, but it was meant literally. What happened was that there was a six-week trial. Television reporters were there drawing pictures of attorneys and all that. It got a lot of attention. Suddenly my status as program idiot changed and I was briefly a star.

> ______ started working on a prison case. There was a period of incubation while he was in discovery and there was nothing in the paper. Nobody knew what he was doing. So for a year or however long it took to get to trial and was making headlines, it was, "What the hell is that guy doing? He doesn't do a fucking thing. What's wrong with him? We could get rid of him and pay two lawyers with his salary. What this program needs is to get rid of people like ______ who make a lot of money and do nothing." After he brought the case, I mean it was, "he's brilliant, he's wonderful, he's terrific."

RECRUITMENT AND TRAINING

Table 24 summarizes important aspects of each program's recruitment and training procedures. In recruiting new personnel, four of the five programs employ as one criterion the attitudes of applicants regarding activity mixes. Policymakers in these programs seek to prevent abrupt changes resulting from personnel turnover by hiring new lawyers expressing attitudes consistent with the program's prevailing mix.

For most of its history, Metro City favored applicants interested in social reform. A new director appointed in the late 1970s is more service-oriented than previous administrators, but he shares hiring authority with a staff committee that continues to favor law reform. One veteran lawyer who sits on the hiring committee described its hiring criteria as follows:

> We pick and choose people who, number one, look like good lawyers. And people who have some commitment to doing something about poverty. We want people with a commitment to impact work. A lot of that is determined by their politics and their interests. If someone says they're interested in tax law, you look at them in the eye and say, "Why do you want to come here?" You know what they're going to do. They're gonna handle nothing but the individual cases and take the least expenditure of time. Doing impact work is hard, its time-consuming. You've gotta devote yourself to it. That's where politics comes into play. If you don't have a political orientation, you won't do it. We want people with this orientation.

Because the new director's preferences are different from many of the staff, conflicts have occurred occasionally between him and the committee over hiring decisions and, as indicated in the remarks of the director and a member of the hiring committee, the programs' more recent recruits have a variety of predispositions.

> (Director): They [the committee] probably would not recommend that a person who is not interested in complex litigation be hired. And more than that, they like you to give them a little speech, something like, "We are social engineers. We are the vanguard of the poor people's struggle." I've seen them pass on people who did not come on strong enough in this regard. I, however, have final authority and have on occasion picked them over individuals who have impressed the committee by coming on with the party line, so to speak.

> (Member of Hiring Committee): We've had situations where the director ignores the recommendation of the hiring committee. This place in the last few years has become a mixed bag as a result. It really has. There are people who've been hired by this director who in the past would not receive serious consideration.

Because there has been little turnover since the new director's ap-

Table 24
Recruitment and Training by Program

	Program				
	MCLS	IRLS	SLS	ReqRLS	RLS
Recruitment					
Purposive recruitment	yes, reform	yes, service	yes, service	no	yes, service
Training					
Skills learned	reform and service	service	service	mixed	service

pointment, a majority of staff still prefer a mix of activity including substantial amounts of law reform. In a program as decentralized as MCLS, the purposive recruitment of lawyers with a desire to bring reform litigation increases the probability that at least a portion of the program's resources will be so allocated.

Administrators in Industrial Region, Suburban, and Rustic favor applicants expressing an interest in service activity. IRLS refuses to hire lawyers wishing to work immediately in the central office, which brings the vast majority of reform suits. SLS rejects applicants hoping to sue established institutions.[6] The director of RLS informs applicants that his program does not engage in law reform and advises them to seek positions elsewhere if they desire to do so. Comments of an IRLS and RLS lawyer and a SLS administrator demonstrate the importance of preferring service for lawyers who wish to be hired by these programs.

(IRLS lawyer): _____ was a law student who worked with _____ on the jail case. He was a very good law student and did a lot of work on it. He essentially wrote one of the briefs. They offered him a job and he said he only wanted to do prison work. At that time, the suit was in full swing and there's any number of prison suits waiting to be brought. So they said to him, "Alright, look, we'll hire you but you have to go to a neighborhood." So unless he could work out some special deal with his managing attorney, he would be able to work on impact litigation only if he could fit it in with his regular caseload. We lose good people that way.

(SLS administrator): The thing we look for more than anything else when I've been involved in the interviewing is somebody that we think will feel comfortable in our concept. . . . I think the idea of individual services to individual clients has been handed down through the history of the program. One of the big things we look for in interviewing somebody, quite frankly, is somebody who we think is gonna be a team player along those lines. I remember one interview we had with a young lady. All she wanted to talk about was who did we sue last month. "Did you sue the county on any housing issues? Did you sue the state? Did you sue the prison?" And I can tell you right now, five minutes into the interview we knew she was not in the running because we just don't feel comfortable with that.

(RLS lawyer): I interviewed with several programs and this program was the only one where your philosophy on impact litigation was not a topic of conversation. _____ [the director] right up front made it known that you weren't gonna do any big impact cases here. He made it known that it was just a service-providing program. It was more or less, "this is the way we are. Take it or leave it."

Although the success of purposive recruitment varied among the three programs, the attitudes of many attorneys in each of them corresponded to the prevailing mix.

Finally, administrators of Regional Rural look with favor on applicants interested in law reform, but they hire lawyers with a variety of predispositions. Their most important criterion is the applicant's previous legal experience, preferably in another legal services program. One administrator explained:

> We ask if the person is interested in doing impact litigation. Now, we'll hire you if you're not, but I think it helps if you show some interest. We look with favor on people who seem to be aggressive and that's one indication of it. . . . But what we really are after is someone who knows the ropes. Someone who knows what it means to work with the poor. Someone who won't go through culture shock. We like to hire lawyers who have worked previously in legal services or legal aid.

None of the programs operate extensive training programs for new lawyers. But because many new attorneys enter legal services fresh from law school, they rely on experienced lawyers within the program for informal training and advice. In IRLS, SLS, and RLS, veteran attorneys teach new recruits the skills needed to engage in service.[7] In IRLS, law reform skills are taught only to attorneys moving from neighborhood offices to the central office. As the remarks of a RLS and SLS lawyer indicate, working with supervising attorneys who have engaged exclusively in individual client service constrains new lawyers who may wish to pursue social reform.

> (RLS): Impact litigation for somebody like me in a rural program that does service work involves a certain fear. It's a fear of the unknown. What do I do? What court do I go to? How do I know I'm doing it right? See, no one here has done this kind of thing. No one can give you pointers. If you've done it twenty times a year or if someone in the program has done it, then you're fairly confident of what judges are gonna do, if they're gonna rule one way or the other. You know the ballpark. But for me, it's like going down to the big city for the first time. You're going to be in awe and a bit confused and generally panicked.

(SLS): When I came in, only ______ did law reform. Now, he didn't really talk much with me until recently. The people I talked with never did large impact cases because they didn't believe in it and really didn't know the first thing about these cases. So I learned what they knew.

In MCLS, and to a lesser extent RegRLS, lawyers informally learn the skills needed for both service and law reform. In RegRLS, new lawyers learn skills of attorneys in the offices to which they are assigned. Since most of its staff primarily engages in service to individual clients, service skills are gained most easily by new recruits. But a few lawyers in the program have brought an occasional reform suit and others may consult with them on particular cases. In MCLS, attorneys in most offices have engaged in law reform and are quite willing to teach their skills to new lawyers. One veteran lawyer described the socialization and training received by new attorneys assigned to his office:

Your first twenty cases . . . would be cases that you co-counsel with an older attorney. You do this till you get your feet wet. Now it so happens that some of what goes on in most offices is major types of litigation. Not all offices, but in most. If you are assigned to one which does it, you would surely be involved in impact litigation, using the kinds of skills you are going to have to use. . . . Ultimately by the end of your first six months or year, you're pretty much weaned from your supervisor in the sense that you now have your own caseload. I encourage the young lawyers to take reform cases on their own after this period. So, there is some pushing, there is some leading the horse to water. Some people don't drink and after awhile you give up on these people.

SUMMARY

Several conclusions emerge from the comparative analysis of organizational characteristics. Two characteristics, caseload size and specialization, seem to have important effects on program activity. Metro City lawyers, for example, allocate a larger portion of their time to reform work than attorneys in other programs in part because they manage lighter caseloads and specialize in one substantive area. Consequently, they are able to identify issues with a potential for reform and have the time needed to prepare and argue complex cases. In Industrial Region and Regional Rural, attorneys manage heavier caseloads and specialize to a lesser extent. Lawyers in both programs engage in law reform, but they are less able to identify reform issues, have less time to devote to them, and consequently allocate less time than Metro City lawyers to reform activity. Finally, Suburban and Rustic lawyers manage heavy caseloads and are generalists. They have difficulty identifying reform issues and little time to devote to them.

Program policies also seem to influence activity. The absence of management-imposed constraints on reform work in Metro City provides lawyers with the freedom to bring potentially controversial cases. In IRLS and RegRLS, administrators impose indirect constraints. Administrators in RLS and SLS directly constrain lawyers wishing to engage in social reform activity.

Performance measures used in MCLS and IRLS influence their activity. In MCLS, lawyers for years reported on their law reform cases to the executive director. Administrators in IRLS allocate resources based on the number of cases handled by lawyers and respect within the program is bestowed on attorneys handling large caseloads.

Policies influencing caseload size—case category exclusions and caseload adjustment—appear to have important effects. MCLS policies permit staff lawyers the time to engage in social reform work. SLS, RLS, and to a lesser extent IRLS do not exclude many cases or allow staff to adjust caseloads. Most lawyers in these programs struggle with heavy caseloads and have little time for law reform. RegRLS has exclusion policies similar to MCLS, but does not use them to engage in reform as frequently. This suggests that although policies reducing caseloads are important for programs engaging in a substantial amount of law reform, they do not ensure it. Thus, while liberal critics of legal services programs are correct in noting the constraints on law reform provided by large caseloads, policies facilitating lighter caseloads will not necessarily guarantee that programs will engage in a substantial amount of law reform.

Finally, recruitment and training of new lawyers also influences program activity. MCLS administrators for many years recruited lawyers willing to engage in law reform and veteran lawyers teach new recruits both service and social reform skills. In IRLS, SLS, and RLS, administrators recruit service oriented lawyers who learn the skills needed to handle the routine legal problems of individual clients. RegRLS hires lawyers with varying perspectives who learn skills possessed by established lawyers in the office to which they are assigned.

NOTES

1. See, for example, Herbert Simon, *Administrative Behavior*, 3rd ed. (New York: The Free Press, 1976).

2. One lawyer in Suburban Legal Services specializes in prison law.

3. In one of its offices, one lawyer specializes in welfare law and only handles cases with welfare issues. The other lawyer in this office specializes in bankruptcy, but handles a small number of family law cases. In a second office, lawyers are less specialized, with each one handling cases in two or three areas. One lawyer in this office, however, only handles the cases of prison inmates.

4. All lawyers were asked to indicate the number of active cases they were handling requiring at least one future action. The highest number of cases, averaging over 100 per lawyer, were handled by attorneys in SLS and RLS. A majority of lawyers in IRLS and RegRLS handled over 80 cases each. Caseloads in these programs are designated as "high," although a few lawyers in both programs handle a smaller number of cases. "Moderate" caseloads are those that average between 40 and 80 cases. "Low" or light caseloads are those that average below 40.

5. According to Robert K. Merton, goal displacement occurs when "adherence to the rules, originally conceived as a means, becomes transformed into an end-in-itself." See Robert K. Merton, "Bureaucratic Structure and Personality," in Robert K. Merton, Ailsa P. Gray, Barbara Hockey, and Hanan C. Selvin, eds., *Reader in Bureaucracy* (New York: The Free Press, 1952), pp. 361–371. For a discussion of goal displacement in other organizations, see Michael Lipsky, *Street Level Bureaucracy* (New York: Russell Sage Foundation, 1980), chapter 4. Also, Susan S. Silbey found a very similar phenomenon in her study of the Massachusetts Attorney General's Office of Consumer Protection. See Susan S. Silbey, "Case Processing: Consumer Protection in an Attorney General's Office," *Law and Society Review* 15 (1980–1981): pp. 849–910.

6. Suburban Legal Services did hire one lawyer, the prison law specialist, with a social reform orientation. He was hired specifically to work with inmates with a clear expectation that reform cases might result. This lawyer explained his hiring in the following comments:

> I think they hired me so that when people like you came around, they could say, "Sure, we do law reform. Go down the hall and talk to ______." I feel like I'm almost a token here.

7. Because only one attorney in SLS engages in law reform, he must seek advice on legal strategy from lawyers outside the program. In an interview, he reported that he often discussed his cases with lawyers from MCLS.

8

THE INTERORGANIZATIONAL POLITICS OF LEGAL ACTIVITY

The analysis presented in Chapter 7 suggests that several organizational features of legal services programs constrain poverty lawyers who wish to pursue social reform. This chapter examines a second set of potential constraints—relationships between legal services programs and organizations in their environment. Legal services programs interact frequently and continuously with a variety of individuals, groups, and organizations, such as other government agencies, funding sources, boards of directors, judges, opposing lawyers, bar associations, political officials, clients, and client organizations. As the case studies of SLS and MCLS presented in Chapters 4 and 5 indicate, these groups often have more than a passing interest in the cases brought and legal strategies employed by poverty lawyers. To what extent do differing relationships between legal services programs and organizations in their environment explain varying activity mixes? Does Metro City Legal Services rely more for critical resources on external organizations encouraging legal activism? Do the programs that primarily engage in service to individual clients rely more on external organizations that prefer it over law reform? The interorganizational perspective suggests that they should.

INTERORGANIZATIONAL RELATIONS

Interviews for this study sought to discover lawyers' views on which organizations in their environment they depended upon for critical resources, and the effect of interorganizational dependency on legal activity. Questions were asked about: (1) the degree of consensus regarding appropriate legal services activity among organizations in each program's environment; (2) the organizations in the environment perceived by program staff as most salient; (3) the resources deemed critical that were controlled by salient organizations; and (4) the demands and preferences expressed by these groups.

Environments of the five programs differ in the degree of consensus among groups regarding preferred program activities. Four programs, IRLS, SLS, RegRLS, and RLS face monolithic environments populated by organizations that favor service over law reform. But as Chapter 5 demonstrated, MCLS's environment is pluralistic, composed of organizations with different preferences. One set, including the local bar association, judiciary, and many political officials, prefers service to individual clients. A second set, low-income community organizations, prefers law reform. In sharp contrast to the other programs, MCLS is able to choose its major source of critical resources from among groups that make competing demands.

In either type of interorganizational environment, program personnel are concerned only with those external organizations that may offer critical resources. Even programs in similar environments may differ on which organizations they perceive as most important; those organizations composing what organizational theorists refer to as the "enacted environment."

Most Metro City attorneys cite low-income community groups as the most important sources of external support. In the other four programs, the local bar association and judiciary occupy a prominent position in the enacted environment. Rustic Legal Services staff perceive their governing board of directors as a significant group. And as Chapter 4 shows, Suburban lawyers are concerned about their relations with the county commissioners.

It is significant that none of the programs include their major funding source, the Legal Service Corporation, in their enacted environment. While previous work in interorganizational theory assumes that money and authority are the two "critical" resources leading to an organization's inclusion in an enacted environment, some of this work provides an explanation for the LSC's exclusion. Pfeffer and Salancik, for example, argue that the degree to which an organization depends on another organization is determined in part by the extent to which the granting organization has discretion over the allocation and use of the resource.[1] Similarly, Virginia Gray and Bruce A. Williams write that dependency on a funding agency is likely to be minimal if the grantor is required by statute to grant money or authority, regardless of the grantee's policies and behavior.[2]

Consistent with these expectations, the national Legal Services Corporation is excluded from the enacted environments of its local grantees because it is required by statute to fund them and its decisions on how to allocate funds among programs are not discretionary, but rather based on a rigid formula. Regardless of their activity, local legal services programs receive an amount of funding that corresponds to the number of poor people in the community they serve. The remarks of one administrator in SLS illustrate the views of legal services personnel toward the national Legal Services Corporation:

> The Legal Services Corporation is important because I deal with them a lot. But they are not the most important. They really can't affect us here. I suppose they could defund us, but other than that they can't really do anything except send me 85,000 memos to do this or that.

Previous theoretical work is less helpful in explaining the inclusion of other organizations in the enacted environments of the five programs. These writings assume that in the absence of dependency on a major funding source, organizations are autonomous. However, interviews for this study suggest that organizations other than the major funding source control resources considered critical by program personnel. The precise nature of these resources varies among programs and falls into several categories.

First, organizations other than the LSC contribute funds to legal services programs deemed critical by staff. Suburban Legal Services, as described in Chapter 4, relies on the county commissioners for a small amount of discretionary funding. While the amount of funding is a small portion of its total budget, the program's director and many of its lawyers consider it critical.

External organizations also control financial resources indirectly, influencing the allocation of program funds received from other funding sources and approving, disapproving, or modifying budgetary requests proposed to other sources. Rustic Legal Service's governing board, for example, is perceived by staff to control critical resources because of its extensive involvement in financial decisionmaking within the program. The board scrutinizes budgetary matters closely and, in sharp contrast to the governing boards of the other programs, questions the judgment of the program's director and formulates alternatives. In the past, the governing board refused to grant salary increases to staff, to accept money from the LSC for additional attorneys and an outreach office, and to approve requested funding increases from the LSC for equipment. One RLS lawyer summarized the crucial role of the program's board:

> The most important group for us is obviously our board. They can have a tremendous influence on how or if this program maintains itself. . . . They have looked with interest on our budget and other decisions and we need to have their support as often as possible.

External organizations control an important political resource, lobbying for continued or increased funding for legal services at the local, state, or national level. As Chapter 5 demonstrates, program staff in Metro City value the political support that low-income community organizations provide, both for legal services funding and in internal political conflicts. In contrast, program personnel in Industrial Region, Suburban, and Regional Rural, perceive the local legal community as important sources of political support. Chapter 4 described the perception among SLS personnel that maintaining salutary relations with the legal community helped to ensure continued county funding. In IRLS and RegRLS, the bar association provided support through the passage of resolutions delivered to state and national political officials. This support is valued by program staff, as shown in the following comments:

> (IRLS): The bar association is important because they pass resolutions in support of legal services. I feel it helps us get our money from the state and national government.
>
> (RegRLS): The bar is crucial for political support. Just recently, I presented a resolution to the bar association asking them to support legal services and

full funding for it. And we got pretty prompt support from them. . . . I don't think that something like that would come from a lot of rural bar associations.

Program personnel also value social resources controlled by external organizations. Several MCLS lawyers value the social support provided by leaders and members of low-income organizations. Attorneys in three programs—IRLS, RLS, and RegRLS—sought the approval and respect of local judges and private attorneys. Some strongly identify with the legal profession and seek the approval of private practitioners on this basis, while others, particularly those working in rural communities, feel that good relations with the legal community are essential for living comfortably in the area. Comments of an IRLS and RegRLS attorney illustrate the legal community's control of social resources:

(IRLS): I want to be viewed as a member of the professional community. So I care how I'm viewed by lawyers and judges around here. I mean, I have the feeling that I went to law school to become an attorney and I want to be viewed as another attorney. I see myself as an attorney first and as a legal services attorney second.

(RegRLS): Our job is much easier here if you do have some kind of relationship with the private attorneys. If we get along with them it makes life easier just living here.

In all of the programs but MCLS, staff attorneys stressed the importance of the legal community for rendering decisions affecting their clients and assisting them in disposing of cases expeditiously. In addition, the opinion of the legal community was important to attorneys who eventually hoped to be employed in the private bar. The brief quotations that follow illustrate the legal community's control of decisional, case processing, and career resources.

(RegRLS, decisions): We have one judge in this county. That's it. You better believe that he's important to us and our clients. And I've learned the game that you've got to bend over backwards to be nice to him because he's the only shot in town.

(IRLS, case processing): We . . . need the judge's cooperation on scheduling. For example, in family court you could spend six hours waiting for a case to be called which is dead time for us. Because of the high volume of cases we have, we might have three cases in family court all scheduled for 9:30. And you need a good relationship with the judge's staff to be able to go in and say, "I have to be in this courtoom with this case, I have to be in that courtroom a little later," and so on.

(RLS, career): The board and the bar are important to many of us because they are doing what we hope to do in the future. If you're ever gonna get anywhere, like I want to get out of here and get a job with a private firm, usually that depends on having some kind of tie or getting to know someone who's gonna help you or put a good word in for you somewhere.

Finally, the Metro City case study illustrates the perceived importance of community organizations for supplying valuable information. Community groups offer information that assists attorneys in identifying problems endemic to the poverty community and aids in their resolution.

What effect does the enacted environment have on legal activity? In each of the programs, a relationship appears to exist between the activity preferences of salient external organizations and the prevailing activity mix. Four programs—IRLS, SLS, RegRLS, and RLS—primarily do service work and rely for critical resources on organizations that encourage such activity. MCLS does a relatively substantial amount of law reform and relies on community groups who prefer it over service.[3]

Thus, for descriptive and analytical purposes, four dimensions of each program's interorganizational environment—the degree of consensus among organizations, the composition of the enacted environment, critical resources controlled by salient organizations, and their activity preferences—are significant. These dimensions are summarized for the five programs in Table 25.

Interviews conducted confirm the explanatory importance of the enacted environment and suggest how environmental demands translate into specific patterns of activity. Programs relying on groups that encourage service over law reform are cognizant of these preferences and consider them seriously when making decisions on legal strategy and action. A few examples illustrate the point.

The Suburban Legal Services case study presented in Chapter 4 indicates quite clearly that program attorneys are prohibited from bringing legal actions against county institutions or prominent residents because they may jeopardize county funding. Lawyers in the

Table 25
Dimensions of Interorganizational Environments by Program

Program	Degree of Consensus	Composition of Enacted Environment	Critical Resources	Activity Preference
MCLS	pluralistic	community organizations	political social informational	reform
IRLS	monolithic	legal community	political social decisional case processing career	service
SLS	monolithic	county executive legal community	direct financial political decisional case processing career	service
RegRLS	monolithic	legal community	political social decisional case processing	service
RLS	monolithic	governing board legal community	indirect financial career social decisional case processing career	service

three nonmetropolitan programs avoid bringing law reform suits and controversial cases before local judges because they fear possible repercussions against themselves and their clients. The director of RLS was warned by prominent members of the local bar that he would be fired by the bar-dominated governing board if program lawyers brought law reform suits. RegRLS attorneys fear generating controversy at the local level, so they avoid bringing social reform lawsuits against local institutions and concentrate their law reform resources on state and national bureaucracies, which are sued in federal court. The influence of the environment on activity is shown clearly in the following comments of a member of RLS's governing board and a RegRLS attorney.

(RLS board member): I don't think that _____ [the executive director] ever had a question in his mind that if in fact he flagrantly went in opposition to the expressed policy of the board that he'd be fired. I don't think there ever was a doubt in his mind. It was very clearly stated by me and I know by others that we would never tell him how to handle a case. But don't get into the class action business.

(RegRLS lawyer): There are difficulties in operating a program in a community like this. We're very isolated up here. There's not much support for us. The support we have does not apply to law reform or anything like that. So as far as controversial things are concerned, we will shy away from them at times.

MCLS attorneys are much less constrained than lawyers in the other four programs. For one thing, they may choose their allies from among groups with different preferences. Having chosen low-income community organizations preferring law reform, they willingly respond to requests for social reform activity. In responding to their requests and developing the skills needed to satisfy them, MCLS lawyers increase their chances of doing law reform.

To summarize, the preferences of organizations composing a program's enacted environment are related to, but not completely determinant of, its activity mix. The amount of time program lawyers devote to law reform and service varies, depending in part on demands made and preferences expressed by external groups perceived to control critical resources. It should be clear that the interorganizational environment is only a partial explanation, as evidenced by the fact that three programs—SLS, IRLS, and RegRLS—devote some of their resources to law reform despite the preferences of groups composing their enacted environment for service activity.

TOWARD AN INTEGRATED MODEL OF LEGAL ACTIVITY

How do elements of the individual-level, organizational, and interorganizational perspectives interact? Can the three perspectives be integrated? Further analysis of interview data suggests significant interactions between elements of the three perspectives.

The analysis presented in Chapter 6 indicated that staff attitudes do not relate directly to activity. But the personal predispositions of program staff exert important indirect effects. In pluralistic interorganizational environments, as in MCLS, staff attitudes guide significant decisions: the selection of groups composing the enacted environment and some of the resources deemed "critical." MCLS attorneys, a majority of whom hold left-of-center, reformist attitudes, selected low-income community organizations as allies from among several competing potential sources of support. Low-income groups pursue goals and hold values that are compatible with those of a majority of MCLS members. Further, the values of MCLS attorneys lead them to treat social and informational resources controlled by community groups as "critical." The link between environment and personal values is expressed clearly by one veteran MCLS lawyer:

> Why in the hell do we spend our time representing groups when we know damn well it's not popular? Well, a lot of us went to law school with a purpose in mind. We wanted to adjust some of the problems in society. We wanted a job that would allow us to promote those ends.... Many of us have a political perspective. Now we're not out to grind our own perspective, as some of the conservatives say. But we work closely with groups that share our concerns about society.

In monolithic interorganizational environments, attitudes cannot affect the choice of groups composing the enacted environment, because no real substantive choice exists. But the preferences of program policymakers in such programs influence its organizational features. For example, the service oriented preferences of directors in SLS and RLS correspond to the preferences of groups in the enacted environment. Consequently, program policies, structure, and procedures encourage service over law reform, reflecting the views of both directors and salient external organizations.

However, in IRLS and RegRLS, the attitudes of program policymakers do not correspond to those of groups in the enacted environment. In IRLS, a majority of lawyers and the program's director hold liberal political values, and many prefer that at least a portion of the program's resources be allocated to law reform. To encourage social reform activity, IRLS has a central office staffed by specialized lawyers on limited client intake. But the nature of the program's enacted environment does not permit a substantial amount of law reform, so attorneys in neighborhood offices, the vast majority of staff in the program, do not specialize and handle large caseloads.

Similarly, attorneys and administrators in RegRLS hold left-of-center political values and prefer that the program engage in some law reform. These views conflict with those of groups in its enacted environment. Agency policies and structure give attorneys the time and capability to do law reform, but they take advantage of the opportunity infrequently because they rely on established groups in the community for support.

Although limitations in the research design and data collected for this study do not permit a precise assessment of the relative explanatory importance of variables, the significance of a program's interorganizational environment cannot be overstated. Looking across programs, it is clear that the nature and preferences of groups in the enacted environment influence, typically quite directly, aspects of the organization's structure, its policies, and the capabilities of attorneys to engage in social reform activity.

The importance of the enacted environment is shown most clearly by comparing two programs—Metro City and Regional Rural—that employ attorneys with similar values and have similar organizational features. A majority of lawyers in both programs hold left-of-center, activist attitudes. Attorneys in both programs specialize, and policies permit them time to engage in reform litigation. But because MCLS lawyers are well-informed about poverty community problems by community groups and may rely on them for political support, they have more opportunities to bring reform litigation and are not required to consider possible political repercussions. In sharp contrast, attorneys in RegRLS are less well-informed about major problems affecting the poor in their communities because no low-income community groups are active. In comparing the reform activity in MCLS to that brought by lawyers in his own program, one veteran RegRLS attorney remarked:

It's much easier for MCLS attorneys to litigate the big issues of the day. They've got the Welfare Rights Organization and Metro City Citizens in Action. They've got a lot of people bringing issues to them. We just don't have that luxury up here.

Even when RegRLS staff identify reform issues, they are less able than MCLS attorneys to litigate because their individual clients are more willing to settle than are MCLS's organizational clients. As one RegRLS attorney put it:

[T]he individual client doesn't want impact litigation. You can explain to them that you want to handle their case as a class action and take it to federal court. It's gonna take two years to resolve. Any client will say, "Are you kidding? Clear up my problem as soon as possible. I don't care if I'm the named plaintiff in some big case that's going to federal court." So I have cases like that. I've had some cases that were either potential class actions or good test cases. But the other side offered a settlement. I put the settlement to my client and of course they grabbed it. So there have been situations where what could have been impact cases fell by the wayside because of my client's position.

And finally, RegRLS staff are constrained in bringing reform litigation by conservative local organizations that provide them with political, social, and decisional resources. Therefore, even though attitudes and organizational features permit law reform activity by both programs, MCLS attorneys are more likely than RegRLS lawyers to use the elements of the organization encouraging law reform to bring policy suits.[4]

SUMMARY AND CONCLUSIONS

The findings of this comparative case study shed needed empirical light on ongoing political debates regarding the activity of programs funded by the Legal Services Corporation. Based on the data collected from the five programs, conservative critics appear to correctly identify a liberal orientation among legal services attorneys. Most of the lawyers in this study hold attitudes that fall to the left of the political spectrum. This is not surprising, given the origins of the national program in the War on Poverty, and the nature of cases handled and types of clients served by poverty lawyers.

However, the assumption of many conservatives that left-of-center attitudes translate directly into social reform litigation is not supported by these data. Left-of-center, activist attitudes manifest themselves in reform oriented legal activity only under certain circumstances; where local programs are surrounded by like-minded organizations that provide needed support. Without such support, lawyers predisposed to engage in law reform are constrained by the preferences of salient external organizations opposing such activity. Moreover, given the paucity of well-organized and politically powerful low-income groups, it is likely that few legal services programs allocate much of their time to social reform activity.[5] Therefore, the findings of this study raise suspicions about many of the criticisms expressed by conservatives, as well as previous research that posits a simple, direct relationship between attitudes and legal activity.

The findings also suggest that left critics of legal services programs correctly identify one major obstacle to social reform activity, time constraints imposed by heavy caseloads. However, administrative arrangements designed to free the time of attorneys, such as case category exclusion policies and caseload adjustment, lead to a substantial amount of law reform only in interorganizational environments conducive to it. Where legal services programs institute organizational procedures permitting or encouraging law reform, but are surrounded by organizations opposed to it, lawyers employ these elements of the organization for social reform purposes infrequently.

In addition to their contribution to ongoing political controversies, the findings have important theoretical implications for studies examining relations and resource dependencies between and among organizations. Previous work suggests that organizations are dependent on other organizations to the extent that the external organization is responsible directly for granting a large proportion of the agency's budget or controls its grant of authority. If an organization does not receive money or authority from external organizations, it is assumed that the organization is unaffected by the preferences and demands of organizations in the environment.

This study demonstrates that legal services programs do not depend on their major funding source, the Legal Services Corporation, but they are far from autonomous. In the absence of federal budgetary control, local programs depend on local organizations for a variety of resources deemed critical. Thus, while money and authority may be the crucial resources producing dependency in some organizations, other resources allocated with discretion, such as political support, respect, information, career assistance, and others, may become salient in organizations receiving funds by formula. This finding is significant, given the large number of federal grant programs operating in this way.

The Metro City case helps to address an important question largely ignored in previous work on organizational behavior. How do organizations choose allies when surrounded by a multitude of organizations with diverse preferences, all of whom potentially could provide critical resources? Certainly, organizational theorists have examined administrative choice, although typically within the context of choosing structural arrangements.[6] John Child's work touches most directly on the questions addressed in this study. He argues that studies of organizational environments fail to account for two types of "strategic choice" made by organizational administrators.[7] In some circumstances, administrators choose the type of environment in which they operate. According to Child, "businessmen may have a choice between new markets to enter, educators may exclude certain subjects from their institution's courses, trade union officials may decide on the bounds of their recruitment policy."[8] In addition, organizations may choose to manipulate their environments to increase the likelihood of their survival. Large business corporations, for example, employ advertising to shape consumer demands and preferences.[9] In summation, Child argues that, "some degree of environmental selection is open to most organizations, and some degree of environmental manipulation is open to most larger organizations."[10]

The Metro City case suggests that one important type of strategic choice is which organization or set of organizations to ally with when embedded within a pluralistic interorganizational environment. Metro City staff chose low-income community groups preferring law reform to service activity. What explains this strategic choice? Child speculates that "ideological values" condition administrative choices regarding the environment. In discussing the relationship between environment and organizational structure, he argues, "when incorporating strategic choice in a theory of organization, one is recognizing the operations of an essentially political process in which constraints and opportunities are functions of the power exercised by decision-makers in the light of ideological values."[11] Data collected from Metro City Legal Services provide empirical support for Child's hypothesis linking ideology with strategic choice. MCLS staff chose to ally with low-income groups sharing their preference for an aggressive and activist program.

Administrators and staff in the other four programs are more constrained than MCLS in their choices because they are embedded in monolithic environments. While ideology permits three programs to engage in some law reform activity despite opposition by external organizations, they are unable to engage in a substantial amount. To summarize, this study suggests that distinguishing between types of environments, whether pluralistic or monolithic, is crucial for understanding organizational activity. The explanatory importance of attitudes, organizational features, and context, as well as the manner in which they interact is conditioned by the nature of the agency's interorganizational environment.

NOTES

1. Jeffrey Pfeffer and Gerald R. Salancik, *The External Control of Organizations* (New York: Harper and Row, 1978), pp. 47–50.

2. Virginia Gray and Bruce A. Williams, *The Organizational Politics of Criminal Justice* (Lexington, Massachusetts: Lexington Books, 1980), p. 27.

3. A recent study of Orange County, California, found dramatic differences in the activity preferences of community organization leaders and leaders of the legal community. Consistent with my findings, this study reported that community group leaders favor social reform activity, while judges clearly prefer individual client service. See James W. Meeker, John Dombrink, and John Song, "Perceptions About the Poor, Their Legal Needs, and Legal Services," paper presented at the annual meeting of the Law and Society Association, Chicago, Illinois, May 1986.

4. Part of the variation in activity between MCLS and RegRLS may be explained by differences in aspects of their objective environments, such as the number of poor people served and the nature of the problems. In addition to having a large number of low-income organizations, Metro City has a far greater concentration of low-income residents than the area served by

RegRLS. It is possible that the problems experienced by the poor in these rural communities are of a distinctly different nature and order than in the large metropolitan area. Unfortunately, limitations in the data collected for this study do not permit a rigorous analysis of this possibility. However, since both programs are located in the same state, the rural poor are probably just as likely as those in Metro City to experience problems with state laws and the implementation of social programs by state agencies. These laws are challenged and state agencies sued much more frequently by lawyers in Metro City.

5. On the decreasing number of low-income advocacy organizations, see Marilyn Gittell, *Limits to Citizen Participation: The Decline of Community Organizations* (Beverly Hills, California: Sage Publications, Inc., 1980), especially chapters 7 and 10.

6. For examples, see Alfred D. Chandler, Jr., *Strategy and Structure: Chapters in the History of the American Industrial Enterprise* (Cambridge, Massachusetts: The M.I.T. Press, 1962), and John Child, "Organizational Structure, Environment, and Performance: The Role of Strategic Choice," *Sociology* 6 (1972): pp. 1–22.

7. Ibid.

8. Ibid., p. 4.

9. See John Kenneth Galbraith, *The New Industrial State*, 3rd ed. (New York: The New American Library, Inc., 1978), pp. 247–248.

10. John Child, "Organizational Structure, Environment, and Performance," p. 4.

11. Ibid., p. 16.

9

LEGAL SERVICES AND EQUAL JUSTICE

Guaranteeing equal justice for the poor in a society characterized by inequality is an aspiration fraught with dilemmas and potential conflict. This final chapter explores the inevitable difficulties of furthering the goal of equality in the civil justice system. It summarizes the findings of the previous chapters by focusing on the inherent political nature of legal services work and offers some thoughts on why politics pervade the operations of local programs. The chapter concludes with a discussion of advantages and limitations of law reform and service to individual clients, and considers various reform proposals.

POLITICS AND LEGAL SERVICES FOR THE POOR

The establishment of the OEO Legal Services Program and efforts to insulate it from political pressure in a quasi-public corporation mark important milestones in ensuring some measure of equality in the civil justice system. Since the program's creation in the 1960s, poverty lawyers have represented millions of low-income clients. However, as this study demonstrates, efforts to promote equality by providing the poor with legal advocates run headlong into political reality, a reality that shapes the type of representation afforded the poor. By its very nature, legal services work involves poverty lawyers in political arenas. Legal services attorneys represent the interests of those with few political and financial resources. Because the activity of poverty attorneys has the potential, however remote, of effecting basic changes in the prevailing distribution of resources, their work inevitably generates concern, if not open hostility, among well-organized, powerful interests. Poverty lawyers, simply because they represent indigent clients in a class-stratified society, have opportunities to challenge the policies and practices of powerful organizations and individuals. It should come as no surprise that established groups employ their power to preclude legal services lawyers from bringing these challenges to court.

The most visible manifestation of these conflicts has occurred on the national level. In response to successful law reform suits brought by legal services attorneys, a variety of political leaders have sought to statutorily control their activity or abolish the program altogether.[1] However, this study suggests that constraints on legal activity imposed by organizations on the local level are at least as significant as national efforts. Judges, private attorneys, bar associations, local political leaders, and others with a stake in the status quo, oppose legal activity that seeks social reform. And because legal services programs in many communities must rely on these groups for a variety of resources, they cannot challenge consistently established practices and institutional arrangements.

While the inherent political nature of legal services work explains why local organizations seek to influence the activity of poverty lawyers, it does not explain their success in shaping it. Why do politics and political pressure at the local level play such an important role in determining activity mixes? Several programmatic features of the Legal Services Corporation help to explain.

Like much congressional legislation, the Legal Services Corporation Act states vague program objectives. Indeed, the only substantive objective identified in the legislation is the provision of "high quality legal assistance."[2] The Act fails to specify how legal services resources should be allocated to achieve "high quality" and thus provides no direction to local programs regarding their operations and activity. In addition, the Legal Services Corporation funds programs by formula without regard to activity, further increasing the discretion of local program personnel.

Taken together, the absence of clear program objectives and the nondiscretionary funding scheme gives local actors broad authority to set priorities and decide how best to allocate scarce resources. In the absence of federal direction, legal services staff and administrators are forced to satisfy local organizations perceived to control critical program resources that are allocated with discretion. Especially in a program like legal services for the poor, which at the national level operates constantly under conditions of budgetary uncertainty, local programs are vulnerable to efforts by powerful local groups to set priorities and define appropriate activity. Consequently, in many communities local organizations effectively encourage service to individual clients and constrain social reform activity. Thus, the LSC's decentralized structure has important implications for the specific interests that shape program activity and the type of legal representation provided the poor.

Students of American politics have long suspected that the level in the federal structure at which decisions are made have consequences for the types of interests that predominate. For example, in his seminal work, *Private Power and American Democracy*, Grant McConnell argues that powerful economic interests with an important stake in maintaining the status quo dominate the political process at subnational levels due to the absence of strong competing political parties that aggregate interests.[3] Less powerful groups representing the interests of the disadvantaged may achieve influence only at the national level, where they have the opportunity to form alliances with like-minded organizations from other geographical regions.

The difficulty for the poor and groups that represent them in achieving influence at state and local levels dramatically affects the interorganizational politics of decentralized social programs, such as legal services for the poor. As we saw in four of the five programs studied, local implementing agencies form alliances and depend for resources on the most powerful local interests. These alliances present serious, perhaps insurmountable, obstacles for programs seeking to achieve meaningful social reform.

LEGAL ACTIVITY AND EQUALITY

Throughout this book, I have sought to describe and explain the mix of service to individual clients and law reform activity engaged in by legal services programs. Since the intention in this study was not to evaluate the performance or activities of legal services lawyers, it cannot provide a definitive or authoritative assessment of which set of activities or which specific mix of activity best serves the poor. To answer this question requires further conceptual work and data collection. Nevertheless, the research provides an opportunity to form some judgments. Indeed, since critics of the Legal Services Corporation often evaluate the program and form judgments about its lawyers with little, if any, empirical information and since reform proposals based on these judgements will continue to be offered, the book concludes with some of my impressions.

Providing attorneys to assist the poor with their routine legal problems is an important step in ensuring some measure of equality in the civil justice system. The programs studied engaging primarily or even exclusively in service to individual clients perform a valuable function in protecting and furthering their clients' legal rights, a function that in many cases was not performed prior to the creation of their programs. For example, lawyers in both rural programs reported that private attorneys filed few bankruptcy actions prior to the establishment of their offices. Private lawyers with ties to local business establishments and banks protected creditors' interests by negotiating payment schedules for debts. Private attorneys in several counties refused to file actions under the state's statute providing women protection from spousal abuse, for fear of upsetting local judges unsympathetic to their plight. And in Suburban County, few indigents proceeded *in forma pauperis* prior to the program's creation because both judges and many private lawyers were opposed to waiving court fees. Therefore, in simply forcing local legal systems and decisionmakers to apply established laws, legal services attorneys provide important benefits to the poor.

There are dangers, however, in emphasizing service to individual clients. Because these programs tend to serve large numbers of clients, and doing so is encouraged by management, the goal of providing high quality legal assistance may be displaced by that of serving large numbers. As evidenced in the evolution of the "numbers game" in Industrial Region Legal Services, attorneys may strive not to protect or further the rights of their clients, but rather to dispose quickly of large quantities of cases. In such programs, attorneys often deal with client problems routinely and perfunctorily.

Moreover, while service-providing offices may play an important role in forcing the implementation of established rules, they do not provide the same scope of legal services as attorneys for more affluent clients. Service oriented programs guarantee the poor equal access to courts in certain substantive areas, but they do not provide the diversity of representation and the full range of advocacy that wealthier clients enjoy.

Of the five programs studied, Metro City Legal Services provides the greatest diversity and fullest range of advocacy for the poor. MCLS attorneys, on average, split their time almost evenly between service and law reform. More significant, law reform as practiced in MCLS furthers the substantive political goals of the poor as a class.

The MCLS case suggests that law reform activity planned in consultation with community advocacy groups increases the ability of the poor to achieve social reform goals in established political fora. Close, ongoing relations between lawyers and groups facilitate the design and implementation of long-term reform strategies. This is significant, especially in courts where decisions are influenced less by the political strength of parties than in legislatures and administrative agencies.[4] Indeed, in Metro City the poor have many advantages in pursuing social reform that previously only powerful interests, such as business and industrial corporations, have enjoyed. For example, Marc Galanter argues that the "haves" are more likely than the poor to achieve reform in courts because they are well-organized, well-financed, and able to become "repeat players."[5] Repeat players establish a continuous presence in courts and are interested in rule changes as well as immediate gains. Unorganized, underfinanced "one-shotters," on the other hand, use the courts only on occasion and are interested exclusively in immediate gains. In other words, one-shotters fail to consider the consequences of their case for future judgments, while repeat players calculate the implications of any particular case for future results. In Metro City, the poor have been transformed or upgraded from one-shotters to repeat players because they are organized and have available federally-funded lawyers whose strategies of litigation they help shape.

In communities served by the other four programs, the poor remain one-shotters. Because one-shotters are more interested in immediate gains than in rule changes, attorneys permitted by management to bring law reform suits are forced to settle cases that, if taken further, have the potential for reform. Moreover, lawyers cannot design and implement long-term reform strategies, experience difficulty in monitoring the implementation of reform victories, and are less able than MCLS attorneys to "educate judges" on the merits of novel legal arguments. In comparing the reform work of IRLS and MCLS attorneys, a welfare specialist in IRLS summarized some of the more salient differences in representing one-shotters and repeat players:

> They've litigated over the years and they've been consistent. They're consistently in court, they're consistently good, and they're consistently arguing the same things. You don't win a case on your brief and your argument, necessarily. You win a case on the judge's predilections. And the judge develops predilections from reading your briefs over the years. And if all your briefs have been consistent and have articulated the same issues and have shown you're sincere, it's bound to rub off on the judge. That's the way institutions work and the way individuals work. And that's what's wrong with this place in its litigation. Ours isn't rational. It's not consistent. What we've done is we've pulled out cases and we've done a remarkably good job with them but they don't lead up to anything. I mean they're all over the place. We've done this, we've done that, we're over here, we let a whole bunch of things go by. There's no pattern. We don't have the kind of litigation docketed that they do. . . . The true tale is looking at the shape of what has come out in welfare and other areas of the law. They've had much more of an impact than we have. We've had some big cases, but they're all over the map. If you look at total impact, they've had a much more total impact on the way the system is run.

Given the advantages conferred on the poor in Metro City compared to those served by the other four programs, what reforms might policymakers enact to encourage a more equal mix of activity? One obvious strategy would centralize the program in a national LSC office that ties funding to program activity. The LSC may reward programs engaging in equal mixes of service and law reform. This strategy, however, poses more problems than it solves.

Even though the LSC's decentralized structure has a clear service bias, there are compelling reasons for maintaining it. The poor throughout the country surely share common problems, but their specific nature and priority vary among communities. In some, low-income housing poses the most serious problem for the poor. In others, welfare problems or the reluctance of judges to grant *in forma pauperis* divorces may be considered most salient. Further, local programs reside in communities with varying political environments that under any circumstances mandate different approaches to advocacy. For example, it would be foolish, if not self-destructive, for a national LSC administration to expect MCLS and SLS—programs serving the poor in vastly different contexts—to engage in similar activity.

In a decentralized setting, what may policymakers do to encourage a more equal mix of activity? The Metro City case provides some guidance. First, policymakers in local programs may recruit activist lawyers. A majority of attorneys in MCLS held left-of-center values and believed in aggressively pursuing reform victories for the poor. Staff lawyers might be required to specialize so they may spot reform issues more easily. Policies may be promulgated on case category exclusions and caseload adjustment that provide staff with time needed to develop complex litigation.

Changing recruitment practices, program policies, and program operating features may provide an important initial step in increasing the amount of law reform pursued by local programs. But, as the interorganizational perspective developed in this book suggests, these measures constitute necessary, but not sufficient conditions for dramatically altering activity. To engage in law reform in the amount and quality of MCLS, programs require the support of organizations in the local community that may assist in developing strategies and have the capacity to ensure the program's continued survival. MCLS could not have engaged in the amount of high quality law reform or generated the political controversy it did without the active support of politically powerful low-income community groups. These groups not only assist attorneys with their work, but equally important, provide the program with political support when it encounters intense opposition from political officials and conservative groups in the community.

The implications of the MCLS case seem clear. To promote a more equal mix of activity and social reform work of high quality, national policymakers must commit resources to building effective low-income community groups. Some possible reforms would permit legal services lawyers to organize the poor and assist their development and/or reinvigorate other organizations, such as community action agencies, and require them to allocate much of their time to community organizing.

These proposals bring us to a major dilemma, perhaps *the* major dilemma of guaranteeing equal justice to the poor. The political prospects are dim for a national policy aimed at organizing the poor or promoting aggressive, reform-oriented legal services programs. The Reagan administration has consistently opposed a national legal services program that encourages local programs to file policy suits against powerful interests and allocating federal funds to programs with the potential to increase the political power of the poor. Given the unequal distribution of power in the United States, one may wonder if any national administration would propose and seek to pass legislation that might serve to alter prevailing power relationships.

Without the support of national political leaders for an aggressive legal services program that works with and helps to develop low-income community groups, the ideal of equal justice will never become an empirical reality. Although equal justice will remain an important symbol to most Americans, business organizations and other traditionally powerful interests will continue to achieve their goals in established fora, largely unchecked by other less powerful organizations.

Alternatives to the LSC proposed by the Reagan administration—*pro bono* services by private lawyers and judicare—will have a far different impact on the poor than the proposals discussed above.[6] Private lawyers lack the specialized knowledge of poverty law necessary to spot issues of general concern to the poor. More significant, private lawyers have no incentive, either financial or political, to pursue time-consuming complex litigation or to work with low-income community groups. Indeed, the findings of previous empirical studies are consistent with the interorganizational perspective developed in this book and suggest that private lawyers will be constrained in their legal work for the poor by established interests in the local community whom they rely on for resources. For example, Stewart Macaulay found that private lawyers in Wisconsin were reluctant to initiate consumer cases because of their direct and indirect ties to local business establishments.[7] Some lawyers faced conflicts of interest because they provided legal representation to banks, lenders, and local car dealers. Others believed that aggressively pursuing a consumer claim would risk the good will of existing and potential clients or endanger their networks of contacts. In a study of rural lawyers, Donald D. Landon reported that community pressures forced private practitioners to reject certain types of cases, such as medical malpractice, sexual abuse, and especially civil rights.[8] Finally, Philip R. Lochner, Jr., found that lawyers he studied who engaged in *pro bono* work initiated few legal actions for their indigent clients and settled most with dispatch.[9] None of the over 150 lawyers he interviewed brought law reform cases.

Thus, private lawyers often have strong personal, professional, and financial ties to local interests. Under these circumstances, indigents may expect no more than out-of-court settlements on narrowly conceived issues and occasional appearances in lower courts. Moreover, if the Reagan administration proposals are adopted, the poor lose any opportunity they now have to upgrade their status in courts from one-shotters to repeat-players.

In conclusion, this study has focused primarily on the initial stage in the process of social reform. MCLS lawyers and the community groups they represent have been able to establish many rights for the poor as a result of law reform victories, but the impact of these victories is frequently unclear. Although they won material victories and community organizations monitored their implementation, it is often impossible to force compliance when legal victories run counter to prevailing power relationships.[10] The enforcement problem is illustrated by the fact that the Metro City Housing Authority repeatedly refused to comply with court orders to improve housing conditions, even subsequent to being held in contempt of court. Therefore, the rights created by legal victories may be most significant not for their direct impact on poverty conditions, but rather as Stuart Scheingold argues, as resources to be employed in an ongoing struggle for implementation and political power.[11] Community groups may use the symbolism of rights established by courts to mobilize political support for their implementation and for their broader political goals.[12] Scheingold writes that, "litigation can politicize individual discontents and in so doing activate a constituency thus lending initial impetus to a movement for change."[13] Ultimately, this may be the most significant contribution poverty attorneys make in the struggle for social justice.

NOTES

1. See the works cited in note 5 of Chapter 1.
2. Legal Services Corporation Act of 1974, 42 USC 2996, section 1001.

3. Grant McConnell, *Private Power and American Democracy* (New York: Vintage Books, 1966).

4. See Marc Galanter, "Why the 'Haves' Come Out Ahead: Speculations on the Limits of Legal Change," *Law and Society Review* 9 (1974): p. 95.

5. Ibid.

6. For discussions of these proposals by a member of the Reagan transition team that proposed them, see Samuel Jan Brakel, "Prospects of Private Bar Involvement in Legal Services," *American Bar Association Journal* 66 (June 1980): pp. 726–728, and "Legal Services for the Poor in the Reagan Years," *American Bar Association Journal* 68 (July 1982): pp. 820–822.

7. Stewart Macaulay, "Lawyers and Consumer Protection Laws," *Law and Society Review* 14 (1979): pp. 115–171.

8. Donald D. Landon, "Clients, Colleagues, and Community: The Shaping of Zealous Advocacy in Country Law Practice," *American Bar Foundation Research Journal* (Winter 1985): pp. 81–111.

9. Philip R. Lochner, Jr., "The No Fee and Low Fee Legal Practice of Private Attorneys," *Law and Society Review* 10 (1975): pp. 431–473.

10. The literature on the problematic impact of court decisions is voluminous. For good reviews, see Stephen L. Wasby, *The Impact of the United States Supreme Court: Some Perspectives* (Homewood, Illinois: Dorsey Press, 1970), and Charles A. Johnson and Bradley C. Canon, *Judicial Policies: Implementation and Impact* (Washington, D.C.: CQ Press, 1984).

11. Stuart A. Scheingold, *The Politics of Rights: Lawyers, Public Policy, and Political Change* (New Haven, Connecticut: Yale University Press, 1974), pp. 83–219.

12. Katz has argued that the major impact of law reform victories achieved by legal services lawyers is in legally segregating the poor from other classes and helping political officials to administer the welfare state. See Jack Katz, *Poor People's Lawyers in Transition* (New Brunswick, New Jersey: Rutgers University Press, 1982), chapter 10, and "Caste, Class, and Counsel for the Poor," *American Bar Foundation Research Journal* (Spring 1985): pp. 251–292. While his analysis may be correct for some of the cases brought by poverty lawyers, he ignores the important symbolic effect of litigation for mobilizing the poor. Katz also ignores other indirect results of law reform litigation, such as changing legal rules that impede political mobilization, providing community groups with political leverage when bargaining with government agencies and other organizations, raising the consciousness of attentive and mass publics, and providing publicity for causes and organizations. On these and other indirect results, see Joel F. Handler, *Social Movements and the Legal System: A Theory of Law Reform and Social Change* (New York: Academic Press, 1978), chapter 6.

13. Scheingold, *The Politics of Rights*, p. 37.

APPENDIX A

METHODOLOGY

This appendix describes the history and methodology of the research upon which this book is based. It discusses the research design chosen, criteria employed in selecting research sites, methods of data collection, and techniques used for data analysis. Subsequent to this discussion, some of the major research instruments employed in this study are reproduced.

RESEARCH DESIGN

In developing this study, a design was sought that balanced the need for reliable, in-depth information on the operations of legal services programs with the desire to identify variables which explain variations in activity. Given the lack of hard empirical information regarding legal services programs, an intensive investigation of a few programs promised to be the most productive method by which to describe activities accurately and develop a model. Therefore, a comparative case study design was chosen, examining five programs of varying size located in settings that differed in several ways.

The comparative case study design seemed appropriate for this study because it possesses many of the advantages of the intensive single-case study and of more extensive comparative designs, such as those employed in survey research. Specifically, it allows for detailed examination of individual cases, an advantage in exploratory research of this kind that seeks to describe and explain complex social processes. Equally important, the comparative case study permits a consideration of cases with variation on key variables, increasing our ability to generalize the findings. Thus, the design chosen for this study enabled me to examine the operations of a few programs in great detail and compare across programs in an effort to identify variables explaining differences in their activity.

SELECTING PROGRAMS FOR STUDY

Five legal services programs located in a single state were chosen for study. In selecting research sites, I sought to maximize differences in size of agency, populations served, and reputed activities. Interviews conducted in the summer of 1980 with national, regional, and state legal services officials and a reading of the most recent LSC evaluations provided information regarding these characteristics. Brief descriptions of the programs studied are presented in Chapter 3.

Admittedly, the sample of programs selected is not ideal. Because only a handful of programs located in a single state were studied, findings cannot be generalized with confidence to programs in other states. However, for exploratory research such as this, the sample had many practical and substantive advantages which outweighed any problems presented. For example, with limited resources, intensive studies of five programs could be conducted. The geographical proximity of the research sites enabled me to complete the research in a timely fashion and deal efficiently with interview scheduling problems.

More important, in focusing on programs located in one state, there was effective control for state-level variation that could easily contaminate the findings. In addition, the single-state design facilitated the interviewing of several respondents, such as state government lawyers and officials, who had extensive knowledge of all programs in the state and the means by which to compare their legal strategies and style of representation.

Selecting programs differing in size and communities served proved valuable in maximizing variation among agencies in the nature of interorganizational relationships. For example, relations between rural programs and external organizations were more frequent, included less actors (e.g., low-income community groups were inactive or nonexistent in the rural communities), and were more informal than in urban and suburban communities. Further, external organizations communicated demands and expectations more clearly to legal services programs in rural communities than in more populous areas.

FIELD RESEARCH AND DATA COLLECTION

Prior to beginning the field research, detailed letters were written to program directors explaining the research and asking for their assistance. I requested a meeting with each director to elaborate on the study's purpose and answer any questions they or their staff had regarding the project. Fearing problems in gaining access to these programs at a time when they were under political attack from the Reagan administration, I felt it desirable to spend as much time as necessary assuring program personnel that I was engaged in a large-scale academic research project, rather than seeking to write a journalistic exposé or an evaluation to be used against them by conservative critics. Thus, during my initial discussions with program personnel, it was stressed that I sought not to evaluate them, but rather to understand how they made decisions on legal strategy. They were also promised anonymity.

The directors of four programs showed enthusiasm for the study from the beginning, offering their support and assistance. One director, however, was extremely cautious initially, but offered support after being assured in writing that the program's name and location would be withheld from research reports. Ultimately, then, all of the directors cooperated, granting interviews, permitting free access to their staffs, and providing documents regarding the operation of their programs (e.g., budgets, policies, lists of law reform cases, minutes of board meetings). The directors of the large metropolitan programs wrote letters approving the project that I could show their staff if necessary.[1]

With only a few exceptions, staff attorneys were extremely cooperative, spending a considerable amount of time speaking about themselves and their jobs. While initially a few were suspicious of the research and the researcher, these feelings typically diminished after a number of interviews had been conducted with other staff lawyers and the interviewer became somewhat of a familiar face in the agency.[2]

However, a handful of lawyers were uncooperative throughout the field visits. One lawyer, for example, refused to participate, stating that legal services programs were "misunderstood" and that "everyone is out to get us." My argument that his participation would enable him to correct these "misunderstandings" proved unpersuasive. Another lawyer interrupted interviews conducted with other lawyers in the agency on three separate occasions, at one point asking incredulously, "Are you talking to *him*?" This lawyer refused to participate on several occasions, giving various reasons for his lack of interest in the project. Finally, after more than 20 telephone calls to him, he agreed to be interviewed, asking that I meet him at his office at 6:30 the following morning! The interview itself was anticlimactic, but differed from others conducted because the respondent criticized nearly every question asked. Fortunately, this experience was an exception to the general rule of staff assistance.

Two major types of research instruments were employed to collect data for this study. First, interview schedules were constructed to be administered to program administrators, staff lawyers, and representatives of organizations that interact with legal services offices. The questions sought to operationalize program activity and the three sets of explanatory variables. A few questions were dropped, others added, and several were modified subsequent to a pretest of the instruments in a rural community that was not part of the study. In all, 184 interviews were conducted. Table A.1 reports the number of individuals interviewed in various roles.

Ninety of the interviews were conducted with legal services program personnel. These were lengthy, lasting from one hour to three hours. Some administrators and veteran staff lawyers were interviewed on several separate occasions to confirm what had been learned and check the validity of what others had stated. Topics covered in the interviews included personal backgrounds, political attitudes, program characteristics (e.g., structure, policies, decision-making procedures, and environment), importance of external groups, and work priorities.

Interviews were also conducted with 75 individuals representing organizations that interact with local programs, such as bar association officials, judges, government agency lawyers, and community

Table A.1
Number of Individuals Interviewed by Role

Role	Number
National/State Administrators	18
Local program personnel	90
Judges	21
Governing board	20
Community organization leaders	14
Bar association officials	6
Government agency lawyers	14
Political officials	1
Total	184

organization leaders. These interviews ranged from 45 minutes to two hours in length and included questions about the organization's relationship with the legal services office, their general assessment of program performance, and avenues available to them to express criticism or praise for program activities.

With only a few exceptions, respondents allowed interviews to be tape-recorded. These tapes were transcribed and analyzed. For the few respondents who refused to be taped, notes were taken and read into a tape recorder as soon as was practicable. Only three individuals refused to participate in the study—the legal services lawyer mentioned previously, a judge, and a bar association official.

A questionnaire was also administered to legal services lawyers. I asked all respondents to complete these at the conclusion of the in-depth interview and waited, usually in an outer office or hallway, for the lawyer to complete it. The questionnaire took approximately ten minutes to complete and asked for information regarding the lawyer's background, legal experience, organizational affiliations, political party affiliation, and political ideology.

All lawyers and paralegals in the rural and suburban programs were interviewed. Because the staffs of the urban programs were quite large, I could not interview everyone. Both of these agencies were large multi-office programs and activities varied among the offices. Therefore, lawyers were selected for participation in the study based on their office location. The total sample of lawyers in each urban agency includes a percentage from any one office location corresponding to the percentage from that location in the entire program.

Representatives of external organizations were identified and selected in a number of ways. First, the literature on legal services suggests that certain groups, in particular the local bar association and judiciary, are important groups that come into daily contact with program staff. Thus, I asked legal services lawyers to name judges they appeared before most frequently and interviewed as many of them as possible.[3] Bar association officials were identified by program personnel, governing board members, or by calling the local bar association headquarters. Other external groups of importance and contacts within them were identified by legal services lawyers in their interviews or by others in the community that I met.

The field research in the five communities took nearly eight months to complete, from August 1981 to March 1982. I spent approximately two months studying one of the urban programs and three months in the other metropolitan area because it included the suburban agency. Approximately six weeks were alloted for field work in each of the rural communities.

DATA ANALYSIS

The exploratory quality of this study prevented the use of sophisticated multivariate methods of analysis. Instead, less rigorous techniques were relied upon to cull relevant information from interviews and organize it in a way that permitted comparisons across programs. The methodology employed does not permit a rigorous testing of hypotheses, but it is appropriate for research that seeks to build an internally consistent, testable theory from a set of loosely stated, relatively unconnected hypotheses derived from previous research.

To measure the dependent variable—program activity—each lawyer was asked in the interview to estimate the amount of time he/

she spent engaging in law reform and service. These estimates were culled easily from interview transcripts and aggregated by program. To measure the mobilization process, lawyers were asked how they informed themselves regarding poverty community problems; their responses were extracted from interview transcripts, and the information aggregated by program. The validity of these data was checked by examining summaries of law reform activity throughout the country reported in the journal, *Clearinghouse Review*, and interview responses of individuals outside the program.

The three sets of explanatory variables were measured with a mix of quantitative and qualitative data. Some of the quantitative data, such as the age of lawyers and the number of years of legal experience, were obtained from the questionnaire. Other data, such as career ambitions of staff, were extracted from interview transcripts. All of the individual-level information was coded on a single sheet for each lawyer and then aggregated by program.

Devising a methodology to analyze the qualitative data and compare across the five programs proved to be quite challenging. Qualitative interview data were sorted by topic, taped to notecards, and filed by topic. This was accomplished by physically reducing pages of the transcribed interviews so that one page could be taped to a 5″ × 8″ notecard. The reduced interviews were read, cut, taped to notecards, and filed by topic. The filing topics corresponded to the three sets of explanatory variables (e.g., relations with external groups, political attitudes, organizational policies) and to areas discussed frequently by respondents (e.g., working conditions, complaints about management personnel).

A variety of intensive techniques were employed to examine interview responses. First, I read all of the interviews from a particular community in one sitting. Then, I examined all of the interviews across programs for a particular role, and finally, I read all of the notecards in each substantive category within and then among programs at one sitting. These techniques served to uncover patterns of activity within and among the five programs and generated hypotheses that may be tested more rigorously in the future.

NOTES

1. The letters discussed the purposes of the study and asked staff to cooperate. The only restriction mentioned in the letters was a reminder to

lawyers to protect client confidentiality. I initially felt these letters would prove useful, but only a handful of lawyers seemed concerned about the director's response to the study. So while I carried these letters with me at all times during the field visits, I rarely showed them to respondents.

2. I was surprised and concerned at the degree of suspicion shown by a few of the lawyers I encountered. One seemed convinced that I was an agent of the F.B.I. sent by the Reagan administration to uncover irregularities. Another called my dissertation adviser to learn more about my background. After being assured that I was indeed engaged in an academic research project, this lawyer began to ask questions about my dissertation adviser's background! Fortunately, these cases are unusual, but they underscore the importance of promising anonymity to programs and staff in order to obtain valid information about their operations.

3. This was not a problem in rural counties because they have only one or a few judges. In these communities, I interviewed all of the sitting judges and a few former judges.

APPENDIX B

RESEARCH INSTRUMENTS

Interview schedules were constructed and administered to individuals filling each of the roles shown in Table A.1. While many of the questions I asked representatives of external organizations were identical, some were role-specific. For example, judges were asked about the program's impact on court caseloads and private attorneys about the effect of the program on their practice and income. In this appendix, interview schedules are included for staff attorneys and one group of external actors, judges. These instruments are reproduced to show the range of questions asked. Also included is the staff attorney questionnaire.

INTERVIEW GUIDES FOR PROGRAM STAFF

I. Questions relating to individual background, career plans, attitudes, hiring process.

1. (To be asked of *both* neighborhood attorneys and those in law reform units): Perhaps you could begin by telling me how and when you happened to come to (*name of program*). (Probe if necessary): How was your job obtained? What role, if any, did personal or political connections play?
(If not covered): What was there about the position that attracted you to it? Anything else? What was there about this particular program that attracted you to it? How long do you intend to stay in the program? What do you intend

to do after legal services? How do you think your experience here will affect your subsequent career?

2. I would like to ask you a few questions about the hiring process here.
   A. Who conducted the interview(s)?
   B. What kinds of questions were you asked? What did the hiring committee (or person) seem most interested in knowing about you?
   C. How did you respond to their questions?
   D. If a friend of yours was being interviewed for a staff attorney position, what kind of advice would you give your friend concerning the interview process?
3. I would like to ask you about your personal feelings concerning the proper role of legal services. Some believe the program should service the needs of individual clients, helping with the day to day problems confronting the poor. Others see the program as properly fighting for broad reform goals.
   A. What is your belief about the proper role of legal services? Why?
   B. Would you say that your belief is in the majority or minority in (*name of program*)?

II. Questions concerning program structure (hierarchical or decentralized).

1. (Ask *both* neighborhood attorneys and those in law reform units): Staff attorneys report wide differences in the amount of discretion they enjoy as opposed to control by management personnel. How would you describe the degree of autonomy granted to you in the handling of cases?

   (Probe as necessary): In what areas is the greatest control exercised? How is control achieved? Are efforts at control in some areas unsuccessful? Where? Why? Where are you granted widest discretion? Does the managing attorney consider himself or herself more as a "first among equals in a law firm of professional partners" or more as a boss who bears the responsibility to oversee the work of subordinates?

III. Questions concerning program operations and program policies.

1. (Ask *both* neighborhood attorneys and those in law reform

units): I'm interested in the way in which you are informed about the most pressing problems in the poverty community. How does this office inform itself about the poor's legal problems?
(Probe if necessary): What role do other organizations or individuals play in identifying problems? (Mention WRO, tenant organizations, clients council.) Do others play a role? Who?

2. What do you see as the most pressing problem in this community?
3. Are efforts made in this program to coordinate legal actions? For example, are attempts made to group individuals with similar legal problems together so that coordinated strategy may be devised to deal with the problem?

For Neighborhood Attorneys Only:

I would like to ask you how you divide your work time.

1. First, what percentage of your time is spent on servicing individual client needs as they relate to common daily problems?
   Could you describe the nature of your service activities? What are the most common problems? How do you handle these problems? How successful are you? How often do you go to court? How are decisions made on when you go to court? Why don't you spend more time on the preparation of test cases or other reform oriented legal work? Could you spend more time on these activities if you wanted to? (If not): Why not?
2. What percentage of your time is spent on law reform (i.e., the preparation of class action suits, test cases)? How are decisions made on when to attempt reform?
   (Probe): Why not more time on law reform? Why not more time on servicing clients?
   (If some time spent on law reform): In the past year, what were your biggest law reform cases? Could you tell me about them? (Ask about parties involved, issues involved, outcome, impact.)
   (If program has law reform unit): How do you decide when to refer a case to the law reform unit?

3. Does your office have a community education program?
   (If yes): Could you describe it? What are its goals? How successful have you been in reaching these goals?
   How much of your time is devoted to community education?
   (If some time): Describe your duties.
4. If you could increase or decrease the amount of time you spend on various aspects of your work, what would you choose to increase?
   Why?
   Anything else?
   What would you decrease? Why?
   What else? Why?

For Attorneys in Law Reform Units Only:

1. Is all of your time spent on law reform?
   (If no): What else do you do?
2. In the past year, what were your biggest reform cases? Could you tell me about them? (Ask about parties involved, issues involved, outcome, impact.)
3. How do neighborhood attorneys decide when to send you a case? Are their any guidelines?
   Do you inform neighborhood attorneys about case types that you are interested in?
   (If yes): Does this normally prompt them to send you the type of case that you are looking for?
   (If not covered): Relations between law reform units and neighborhood offices are sometimes very cooperative and sometimes conflictual. How about here?
   (Probe): When are you likely to cooperate? When is conflict likely? Do you ever feel that neighborhood attorneys are not sending you all of the cases with potential for reform? (If so): Why do you think they do not?
4. If you could increase or decrease the amount of time you spend on various aspects of your work, what would you choose to *increase*? Why?
   Anything else?
   What would you decrease? Why?
   Anything else? Why?

For Both Neighborhood and Law Reform Attorneys:

Now I would like to ask you about any office policies that affect the way you do work.

1. Does your office have any policies regarding the bringing of class action suits?
   (Probe as necessary): Is clearance of superiors or others (governing board) required? Who makes final decisions on class actions?
   (If no policy): How do you decide when to bring a class action suit? Has this office brought one in the past year? (If yes): Could you tell me about it?
2. Does your office have any policies regarding appeals?
   (Probe as necessary): Is clearance of superiors or anyone else needed? Who makes final decisions on appeals?
   (If no policy): How do you decide when to appeal? Has this office appealed a lower court decision in the past year? Could you tell me about the case(s)?

For Neighborhood Attorneys Only:

1. Does your office have any policies regarding limiting the caseload (i.e., turning away clients)?
   (Probe): Under what conditions will the caseload be limited? Has the caseload ever been limited? When? Why?
2. What about policies on client referrals to private attorneys?
   (Probe): When will you refer? What procedures are used to direct the client to another attorney?

For Both Neighborhood and Law Reform Attorneys:

3. How many cases do you typically have open at one one time? How does the size of your caseload affect your work?

IV. Questions concerning interorganizational relations.

1. (Ask both neighborhood and law reform attorneys):
   As part of your job, you must come into contact with many outside groups and organizations.
   A. Could you mention the groups and organizations that you interact with as part of your job? (Let the respondent talk; probe for clarification. As necessary, probe or prompt with the following questions):
   B. Whose cooperation and support are more important to

you? (If some of this has been covered, say: You talked about the importance of [whomever]. Who else is it especially important to get along with?)

Why is it important to have the cooperation and support of (relevant actor)?

C. Who are the critical people who evaluate, criticize, and praise your work in this community?

(If any of the following are not mentioned,) ask: What about

(1) Your colleagues in the office?
(2) Superiors in the program?
(3) The LSC Regional Office of National Office/Board?
(4) Legal Service Center or its board?
(5) The State Legislature?
(6) Judges?
(7) Community organizations? (If yes): Which ones?
(8) Government agency personnel? (If yes): Which agencies?
(9) Bar association officials?
(10) Private attorneys?
(11) Governing board?
(12) (Local funding source)?
(13) Local elected officials?
(14) Clients council?

(As appropriate, ask about those of the above that respondent ranks as important):

D. What are (appropriate actor) looking for when they evaluate your work? What do they want you to do? What do they not want you to do?

E. What is there about (appropriate actor) that makes their evaluation relevant and important to you?

F. How does the fact that these organizations evaluate your work affect the way in which you handle cases?

G. How would this organization react to a suit against a government agency?

Law Reform efforts?

If I asked people in this organization what the role of the LSC should be, what do you think they would say?

H. (Ask about groups not mentioned as important): Why

don't you consider this organization to be important?

INTERVIEW GUIDE FOR JUDGES

1. How often do you hear cases involving a person represented by an attorney from *name of program*? About how many cases per year?
2. I am interested in your assessment of the program and its attorneys.
   A. First, in what major ways, if any, do legal service attorneys differ from private attorneys?
      (Probe): Ask About: attorney performance
      type of cases brought to court
      tactics in litigation
      amount of time it takes to dispose of a case
   B. What do you see as the strong points of the program?
   C. What aspects of the program are you least satisfied with?
   D. What, if anything, can you personally do to express your dissatisfaction? Have you ever done this? With what result?
3. More generally, I am interested in your assessment of federally funded legal services.
   A. What is your opinion of using federal funds to supply indigents with legal assistance? Why?
   B. Is there a better way to provide assistance? (If yes): What would this program look like?
      (If not covered earlier): Some people believe that legal services should press broad reform goals, relying on class action, law reform, and lobbying strategies. Others believe the program should handle the day to day problems of individual clients.
      What is your view of the role of legal services?
      What role does *name of program* assume?
4. Next, I am interested in some of your actions and policies that may affect the *name of program* and their clients.
   A. First, do you ever refer people to the program?
      (If so): How often? What type of cases? Are there oc-

casions when you do not refer a person that would meet eligibility requirements? Why not?

B. What is your general policy regarding the granting of *in forma pauperis* petitions?
When will you grant?
When will you not grant?
Does this program file for these petitions too often, too little, or about the right amount of time?

5. Finally, I am interested in what impact *name of program* has had on court operations.

A. Has the program affected the way in which you do your work? Have you had to change anything?
(Ask about): increased caseloads, court delay.

B. Have judges, yourself included, affected the way in which legal service attorneys handle cases? In what ways?

BACKGROUND QUESTIONNAIRE FOR LOCAL PROGRAM PERSONNEL

1. In what year were you born? __________

2. How many years have you lived in this community?

   ____

3. If you are not a life long resident of this county, has your residence here largely coincided with your professional career?

   Yes_____ No_____ Life long resident_____

4. From what college or university did you receive your undergraduate degree? ________________________________

5. From what law school did you graduate? _____________

   ____

6. What year did you graduate? __________

7. Since you have been in your present position have you been a member or officer of:

	Member		Officer	
	Yes	No	Yes	No
American Bar Association	___	___	___	___
State Bar Association	___	___	___	___
County Bar Association	___	___	___	___
American Judicature Society	___	___	___	___
Trial Lawyers Association	___	___	___	___
NLADA	___	___	___	___
American Civil Liberties Union	___	___	___	___

National Lawyer's Guild ___ ___ ___ ___

A national association of lawyers not listed above ___ ___ ___ ___

A nonnational association of lawyers listed above ___ ___ ___ ___

8. How many of the following organizations do you belong to?

   a. Veterans Organizations (American Legion, VFW, Amvets, etc.) ______________________

   b. Religious organizations (Knights of Columbus, B'nai B'rith, etc.) ______________________

   c. Service organizations (Elks, Lions, Kiwanis, Masons, etc.) ______________________

   d. Business organizations (Chamber of Commerce, Junior Chamber of Commerce) ______________________

9. Which of the following best describes your partisan preference?

   strong Republican ______

   average Republican ______

   weak Republican ______

   Independent ______

   weak Democrat ______

   average Democrat ______

   strong Democrat ______

   other ______

10. Which of the following best describes your political beliefs?

conservative	______
moderate conservative	______
middle-of-the-road	______
liberal	______
left-liberal	______
left-radical	______

BIBLIOGRAPHY

BOOKS

Aldrich, Howard E. *Organizations and Environments*. Englewood Cliffs, New Jersey: Prentice-Hall, 1979.

Auerbach, Jerold S. *Unequal Justice: Lawyers and Social Change in Modern America*. New York: Oxford University Press, 1976.

Brownell, Emery. *Legal Aid in the United States*. Rochester, New York: Lawyers Cooperative Publishing Co., 1951.

———. *Supplement*. Rochester, New York: Lawyers Cooperative Publishing Co., 1961.

Cappelletti, Mauro; Gordley, James; and Johnson, Earl, Jr. *Toward Equal Justice: A Comparative Study of Legal Aid in Modern Societies*. Dobbs Ferry, New York: Oceana Publications, Inc., 1975.

Champagne, Anthony and Harpham, Edward J. *The Attack on the Welfare State*. Prospect Heights, Illinois: Waveland Press, Inc., 1984.

Chandler, Alfred D., Jr. *Strategy and Structure: Chapters in the History of the American Industrial Enterprise*. Cambridge, Massachusetts: The M.I.T. Press, 1962.

Corsi, Jerome R. *Judicial Politics: An Introduction*. Englewood Cliffs, New Jersey: Prentice-Hall, Inc., 1984.

Curran, Barbara A.; Rosich, Katherine J.; Carson, Clara N.; and Puccetti, Mark C. *The Lawyer Statistical Report: A Statistical Profile of the U.S. Legal Profession in the 1980s*. Chicago, Illinois: American Bar Foundation, 1985.

Donovan, John C. *The Politics of Poverty*. New York: Pegasus, 1967.

Fellman, David. *The Defendant's Rights Today*. Madison, Wisconsin: The University of Wisconsin Press, 1976.

Galbraith, John Kenneth. *The New Industrial State*. 3rd ed. New York: The New American Library, Inc., 1978.

Gittell, Marilyn. *Limits to Citizen Participation: The Decline of Community Organizations*. Beverly Hills, California: Sage Publications Inc., 1980.

Goodman, Leonard H. and Walker, Margaret H. *The Legal Services Program: Resource Distribution and the Low Income Population*. Washington, D.C.: Bureau of Social Science Research, Inc., 1975.

Gray, Virginia and Williams, Bruce A. *The Organizational Politics of Criminal Justice*. Lexington, Massachusetts: Lexington Books, 1980.

Handler, Joel F. *Social Movements and the Legal System: A Theory of Law Reform and Social Change*. New York: Academic Press, 1978.

________; Hollingsworth, Ellen Jane; and Erlanger, Howard S. *Lawyers and the Pursuit of Legal Rights*. New York: Academic Press, 1978.

Heinz, John P. and Laumann, Edward O. *Chicago Lawyers: The Social Structure of the Bar*. New York: Russell Sage Foundation and American Bar Foundation, 1982.

Hurst, James Willard. *Law and the Conditions of Freedom in the Nineteenth-Century United States*. Madison, Wisconsin: The University of Wisconsin Press, 1956.

Johnson, Charles A. and Canon, Bradley C. *Judicial Policies: Implementation and Impact*. Washington, D.C.: CQ Press, 1984.

Johnson, Earl, Jr. *Justice and Reform: The Formative Years of the American Legal Services Program*. New Brunswick, New Jersey: Transaction Books, 1978.

Katz, Jack. *Poor People's Lawyers in Transition*. New Brunswick, New Jersey: Rutgers University Press, 1982.

Lipsky, Michael. *Street Level Bureaucracy*. New York: Russell Sage Foundation, 1980.

McCloskey, Robert G., ed. *Essays in Constitutional Law*. New York: Alfred A. Knopf, 1957.

McConnell, Grant. *Private Power and American Democracy*. New York: Vintage Books, 1966.

Merton, Robert K.; Gray, Ailsa P.; Hockey, Barbara; and Selvin, Hanan C., eds. *Reader in Bureaucracy*. New York: The Free Press, 1952.

Miller, Arthur Selwyn. *The Supreme Court and American Capitalism*. New York: The Free Press, 1968.

Milner, Murray, Jr. *Unequal Care: A Case Study of Interorganizational Relations in Health Care*. New York: Columbia University Press, 1980.

Moynihan, Daniel Patrick. *Maximum Feasible Misunderstanding*. New York: The Free Press, 1969.

Newmyer, R. Kent. *The Supreme Court Under Marshall and Taney*. Arlington Heights, Illinois: AHM Publishing Corporation, 1968.

Pfeffer, Jeffrey and Salancik, Gerald R. *The External Control of Organizations*. New York: Harper and Row, 1978.

Radzinowitz, Leon. *Ideology and Crime*. New York: Columbia University Press, 1966.

Scheingold, Stuart A. *The Politics of Rights: Lawyers, Public Policy, and Political Change*. New Haven, Connecticut: Yale University Press, 1974.

Simon, Herbert. *Administrative Behavior*. 3rd ed. New York: The Free Press, 1976.

Smith, Reginald Heber. *Justice and the Poor*. New York: Carnegie Foundation, 1919.

Stumpf, Harry. *Community Politics and Legal Services*. Beverly Hills, California: Sage Publications, 1975.

Thompson, James D. *Organizations in Action*. New York: McGraw-Hill Book Company, 1967.

Wasby, Stephen L. *The Impact of the United States Supreme Court: Some Perspectives*. Homewood, Illinois: Dorsey Press, 1970.

Weisbrod, Burton A.; Handler, Joel F.; and Komesar, Neil K., eds. *Public Interest Law: An Economic and Institutional Analysis*. Berkeley, California: University of California Press, 1978.

Wildavsky, Aaron. *The Politics of the Budgetary Process*. 3rd ed. Boston: Little, Brown and Company, 1982.

ARTICLES

Agnew, Spiro. "What's Wrong with the Legal Services Program." *American Bar Association Journal* 58 (1972): 930–932.

Aldrich, Howard E. "Resource Dependence and Interorganizational Relations: Local Employment Service Offices and Social Services Sector Organizations." *Administration and Society* 7 (1976): 419–454

Arnold, Mark. "The Knockdown, Drag-Out Battle Over Legal Services." *Juris Doctor* (April 1973): 4–10.

________. "The Odyssey of Legal Services and the Games Politicians Play." *Juris Doctor* (October 1974): 23–28.

________. "And Finally, 342 Day Later." *Juris Doctor* (September 1975): 32–38.

Bellow, Gary. "Turning Solutions into Problems: The Legal Aid Experience." *NLADA Briefcase* (August 1977): 106–107.

Benson, J. Kenneth. "The Interorganizational Network as a Political Economy." *Administrative Science Quarterly* 20 (1975): 229–248.

Berk, Richard. "Champagne's Assessment of Legal Services Programs: An Evaluation of an Evaluation." *Urban Affairs Quarterly* 9 (1974): 490–509.

Black, Donald J. "The Mobilization of Law." *The Journal of Legal Studies* 2 (1973): 125–149.

Brakel, Samuel Jan. "Prospects of Private Bar Involvement in Legal Services." *American Bar Association Journal* 66 (June 1980): 726–728.

________. "Legal Services for the Poor in the Reagan Years." *American Bar Association Journal* 68 (July 1982): 820–822.

Brill, Harry. "The Uses and Abuses of Legal Assistance." *The Public Interest* 31 (1973): 38–55.

Cahn, Edgar S. and Cahn, Jean C. "The War on Poverty: A Civilian Perspective." *Yale Law Journal* 73 (1964): 1317–1352.

Carlin, Jerome E. "Store Front Lawyers in San Francisco." *Trans-Action* (April 1970): 64–74.

________ and Howard, Jan. "Legal Representation and Class Justice." *UCLA Law Review* 12 (1965): 408–418.

________; ________; and Messinger, Sheldon L. "Civil Justice and the Poor: Issues for Sociological Research." *Law and Society Review* 1 (1966): 9–91.

Champagne, Anthony. "An Evaluation of the Effectiveness of the OEO Legal Services Program." *Urban Affairs Quarterly* 9 (1974): 465–489.

________. "The Internal Operations of OEO Legal Services Projects." *Journal of Urban Law* 51 (1974): 649–664.

________. "Lawyers and Government Funded Legal Services." *Villanova Law Review* 21 (1976): 860–875.

Child, John. "Organizational Structure, Environment, and Performance: The Role of Strategic Choice." *Sociology* 6 (1972): 1–22.

Clark, Burton. "Interorganizational Patterns in Education." *Administrative Science Quarterly* 10 (1965): 224–327.

Cook, Karen S. "Exchange and Power in Networks of Interorganizational Relations." *Sociological Quarterly* 18(1977): 62–82.

Cramton, Roger C. "Crisis in Legal Services for the Poor." *Villanova Law Review* 26 (1981): 521–558.

Duncan, Robert B. "Characteristics of Organizational Environments and Perceived Environmental Uncertainty." *Administrative Science Quarterly* 17 (1972): 313–327.

Emery, F. E. and Trist, E. L. "The Causal Texture of Organizational Environments." *Human Relations* 18 (1965): 21–32.

Erlanger, Howard S. "Social Reform Organizations and Subsequent Careers of Participants: A Follow-Up Study of Early Participants in the OEO Legal Services Program." *American Sociological Review* 42 (1977): 233–248.

———. "Lawyers and Neighborhood Legal Services: Social Backgrounds and the Impetus for Reform." *Law and Society Review* 12 (1978): 253–274.

Falk, Jerome B. and Pollack, Stuart R. "Political Interference with Public Lawyers: The CRLA Controversy and the Future of Legal Services." *Hastings Law Journal* 24 (1973): 599–646.

Finman, Ted. "OEO Legal Services Programs and the Pursuit of Social Change: The Relationship Between Program Ideology and Program Performance." *Wisconsin Law Review* (1971): 1001–1084.

Galanter, Marc. "Why the 'Haves' Come Out Ahead: Speculations on the Limits of Legal Change." *Law and Society Review* 9 (1974): 95–160.

George, Warren. "Development of the Legal Services Corporation." *Cornell Law Review* 61 (1976): 681–730.

Hall, Richard H.; Clark, John P.; Giordano, Peggy C.; Johnson, Paul V.; and Van Roekel, Martha. "Patterns of Interorganizational Relationships." *Administrative Science Quarterly* 22 (1977): 457–474.

Hannon, Phillip J. "The Leadership Problem in the Legal Services Program." *Law and Society Review* 4 (1969): 235–253.

———. "Law Reform Enforcement at the Local Level: A Legal Services Case Study." *Journal of Public Law* 19 (1970): 23–48.

———. "The Murphy Amendments and the Response of the Bar: An Accurate Test of Political Strength." *NLADA Briefcase* (April 1970): 163–169.

———. "From Politics to Reality: An Historical Perspective of the Legal Services Corporation." *Emory Law Journal* 25 (1976): 639–654.

Hostetler, Zena. "A Look at Dan J. Bradley." *District Lawyer* (November/December 1980): 56–63.

Houseman, Alan W. "Legal Services and Equal Justice for the Poor: Some Thoughts on Our Future." *NLADA Briefcase* (March 1978): 44–64.

Jurkovich, Ray. "A Core Typology of Organizational Environments." *Administrative Science Quarterly* 19 (1974): 380–394.

Karabian, Walter. "Legal Services for the Poor: Some Political Observations." *University of San Francisco Law Review* 6 (1972): 253–265.

Katz, Jack. "Lawyers for the Poor in Transition: Involvement, Reform, and the Turnover Problem in the Legal Services Program." *Law and Society Review* 12 (1978): 274–300.

———. "Caste, Class, and Counsel for the Poor." *American Bar Foundation Research Journal* (1985): 251–292.

Krislov, Samuel. "The OEO Lawyers Fail to Constitutionalize a Right to Welfare: A Study in the Uses and Limits of the Judicial Process." *Minnesota Law Review* 58 (1973): 211–245.

Landon, Donald D. "Clients, Colleagues, and Community: The Shaping of Zealous Advocacy in Country Law Practice." *American Bar Foundation Research Journal* (1985): 81–111.

Larson, E. R. "Civil Rights Attorneys' Fees Award Act of 1976." *Clearinghouse Review* 10 (1977): 778–781.

Levine, Sol and White, Paul E. "Exchange as a Conceptual Framework for the Study of Interorganizational Relationships." *Administrative Science Quarterly* 5 (1961): 583–601.

Lochner, Philip R., Jr. "The No Fee and Low Fee Legal Practice of Private Attorneys." *Law and Society Review* 10 (1975): 431–473.

Macaulay, Stewart. "Lawyers and Consumer Protection Laws." *Law and Society Review* 14 (1979): 115–171.

Marrett, Cora Bagley. "On the Specification of Interorganizational Dimensions." *Sociology and Social Research* 56 (1971): 83–99.

Mayhew, Leon H. "Institutions of Representation: Civil Justice and the Public." *Law and Society Review* 10 (1975): 401–429.

Menkel-Meadow, Carrie and Meadow, Robert G. "Resource Allocation in Legal Services: Individual Attorney Decisions in Work Priorities." *Law and Policy Quarterly* 5 (1983): 237–256.

Michelman, Frank I. "Foreword: On Protecting the Poor Through the Fourteenth Amendment." *Harvard Law Review* 83 (1970): 7–59.

Note. "Neighborhood Law Offices: The New Wave in Legal Services for the Poor." *Harvard Law Review* 80 (1967): 805–850.

Note. "The Legal Services Corporation: Curtailing Political Interference." *Yale Law Journal* 81 (1971): 231–286.

Note. "Depoliticizing Legal Aid: A Constitutional Analysis of the Legal Services Corporation Act." *Cornell Law Review* 61 (1976): 734–776.

Note. "Developments in the Law—Class Action." *Harvard Law Review* 89 (1976): 1318–1644.

Note. "Civil Rights Attorneys' Fees Act of 1976." *St. John's Law Review* 52 (Summer 1978): 562–593.

Pfeffer, Jeffrey. "Merger as a Response to Organizational Interdependence." *Administrative Science Quarterly* 17 (September 1973): 382–392.

_______ and Nowak, Phillip. "Joint Ventures and Interorganizational Dependence." *Administrative Science Quarterly* 21 (September 1976): 398–418.

Phillips, Howard. "Legal Services Should Not be Federally Funded." *Conservative Digest* (July 1980): 31–32.

Pious, Richard. "Policy and Public Administration: The Legal Services Program in the War on Poverty." *Politics and Society* 1 (May 1971): 365–391.

_______. "Congress, the Organized Bar, and the Legal Services Program." *Wisconsin Law Review* (1972): 418–446.

Pye, A. Kenneth. "The Role of Legal Services in the Anti-Poverty Program." *Law and Contemporary Problems* 31 (1966): 211–249.

Robb, John R. "Controversial Cases and the Legal Services Program." *American Bar Association Journal* 56 (1970): 329–331.

Schmidt, Stuart M. and Kochan, Thomas A. "Interorganizational Relationships: Patterns and Motivations." *Administrative Science Quarterly* 22 (1977): 220–235.

Silbey, Susan S. "Case Processing: Consumer Protection in an Attorney General's Office." *Law and Society Review* 15 (1980–1981): 849–910.

Silver, Carol Ruth. "The Imminent Failure of Legal Services for the Poor: Why and How to Limit Caseloads." *Journal of Urban Law* 46 (1969): 217–248.

Stumpf, Harry. "Law and Poverty: A Political Perspective." *Wisconsin Law Review* (1968): 694–733.

——— and Janowitz, Robert J. "Judges and the Poor: Bench Responses to Federally Funded Legal Services." *Stanford Law Review* 21 (1969): 1058–1076.

———; Schroerluke, Henry P.; and Dill, Forrest D. "The Legal Profession and Legal Services: Explorations in Local Bar Politics." *Law and Society Review* 6 (1971): 47–67.

Sullivan, Lawrence A. "Law Reform and the Legal Services Crisis." *California Law Review* 59 (1971): 1–28.

Terreberry, Shirley. "The Evolution of Organizational Environments." *Administrative Science Quarterly* 12 (1968): 590–613.

Thompson, James D. and McEwen, William J. "Organizational Goals and Environment: Goal-Setting as an Interaction Process." *American Sociological Review* 23 (1958): 23–31.

NEWSPAPERS

Taylor, Stuart, Jr. "Legal Aid Executive Quits, Citing Differences with Reagan's Board." *New York Times*, December 3, 1982, p. A24.

Taylor, Stuart, Jr. "Reagan Withdraws 9 Nominees to Legal Unit." *New York Times*, December 9, 1982, p. A21.

Thornton, Mary and Earley, Pete. "Inside the Legal Services Corporation." *Washington Post*, March 5, 1984, p. A21.

GOVERNMENT REPORTS AND DOCUMENTS

13 *Congressional Record*, pt. 21, at page 27871.

120 *Congressional Record*, at page H7371, 1974.

Economic Opportunity Amendments of 1966. Section 211–1 (b), Public Law 89–794, November 8, 1966, 80 Stat. 1472.

Legal Services Corporation. *Annual Report, 1977.*

________. *Annual Report, 1978.*

________. *Annual Report, 1979.*

________. *Annual Report, 1980.*

________. *The Delivery Systems Study: A Policy Report to the Congress and President of the United States.* Washington, D.C. (June 1980).

________. *Annual Report, 1981.*

MISCELLANEOUS PRINTED SOURCES

Champagne, Anthony. *Legal Services: An Exploratory Study of Effectiveness.* Beverly Hills, California: Sage Professional Paper, Administrative and Policy Studies Series, volume 3, 1976.

Heritage Foundation. *Mandate for Leadership: Project Team Report on the Poverty Aqencies* (October 22, 1980).

Kessler, Mark. "The Interorganizational Politics of Legal Services Agencies." Ph.D. dissertation, Pennsylvania State University, 1985.

McCarthy, Carl Patrick. "The Consequences of Legal Advocacy: OEO's Lawyers and the Poor." Ph.D. dissertation, University of California, Berkeley, 1974.

Meadow, Robert G. and Menkel-Meadow, Carrie. "The Origins of Political Commitment: Background Factors and Ideology Among Legal Services Attorneys." Paper presented at the annual meeting of the Law and Society Association, Toronto, Canada (June 3, 1982).

Meeker, James W.; Dombrink, John; and Song, John. "Perceptions About the Poor, Their Legal Needs, and Legal Services." Paper presented at the annual meeting of the Law and Society Association, Chicago, Illinois (May 1986).

INDEX

About the Author

MARK KESSLER is Assistant Professor of Political Science at Bates College in Lewiston, Maine. He has contributed articles to *Research in Law and Policy Studies*, *Law & Policy*, and *Administration & Society*.